Cambridge Elements

Elements in Econophysics
edited by
Rosario Nunzio Mantegna
University of Palermo
Bikas K. Chakrabarti
Saha Institute of Nuclear Physics
Mauro Gallegati
Polytechnic University of Marche, Ancona
Irena Vodenska
Boston University

THE RISE OF ECONOPHYSICS

A Connected History of Two Disciplines

Gianfranco Tusset
University of Padua

Shaftesbury Road, Cambridge CB2 8EA, United Kingdom

One Liberty Plaza, 20th Floor, New York, NY 10006, USA

477 Williamstown Road, Port Melbourne, VIC 3207, Australia

314–321, 3rd Floor, Plot 3, Splendor Forum, Jasola District Centre,
New Delhi – 110025, India

Cambridge University Press is part of Cambridge University Press & Assessment,
a department of the University of Cambridge.

We share the University's mission to contribute to society through the pursuit of
education, learning and research at the highest international levels of excellence.

www.cambridge.org
Information on this title: www.cambridge.org/9781009671453
DOI: 10.1017/9781009439466

© Gianfranco Tusset 2026

This publication is in copyright. Subject to statutory exception and to the provisions
of relevant collective licensing agreements, no reproduction of any part may take
place without the written permission of Cambridge University Press & Assessment.

When citing this work, please include a reference to the DOI 10.1017/9781009439466

First published 2026

A catalogue record for this publication is available from the British Library

*A Cataloging-in-Publication data record for this Element is available
from the Library of Congress*

ISBN 978-1-009-67145-3 Hardback
ISBN 978-1-009-43943-5 Paperback
ISSN 2754-6071 (online)
ISSN 2754-6063 (print)

Cambridge University Press & Assessment has no responsibility for the persistence
or accuracy of URLs for external or third-party internet websites referred to in this
publication and does not guarantee that any content on such websites is, or will remain,
accurate or appropriate.

For EU product safety concerns, contact us at Calle de José Abascal, 56, 1°, 28003
Madrid, Spain, or email eugpsr@cambridge.org

The Rise of Econophysics

A Connected History of Two Disciplines

Elements in Econophysics

DOI: 10.1017/9781009439466
First published online: March 2026

Gianfranco Tusset
University of Padua
Author for correspondence: Gianfranco Tusset, gianfranco.tusset@unipd.it

Abstract: Classical mechanics provided the conceptual and methodological foundations of neoclassical economics, which has its roots in economic individualism. Since the early twentieth century, statistical mechanics has underpinned a lesser-known approach to economics and finance, one that focuses on aggregates and the interactions between individuals. This has led to the emergence of a new field of research, known as econophysics, which brings to the fore concepts such as emergent properties, power laws, networks, entropy and multifractality, thereby reshaping economic enquiry.

Keywords: econophysics, history, statistical mechanics, aggregates, interactions

© Gianfranco Tusset 2026

ISBNs: 9781009671453 (HB), 9781009439435 (PB), 9781009439466 (OC)
ISSNs: 2754-6071 (online), 2754-6063 (print)

Contents

Introduction	1
Part I **A Long Road (1896–2000)**	4
1 The Fundamentals	4
2 Early Attempts to Use Statistical Mechanics in Economics	14
3 A New Discipline on the Way	20
Part II **A Quarter-Century of Econophysics (1999–2023)**	30
4 Econophysics in a Scatter Plot	30
5 1999–2007: Macroscopic and Microscopic Perspectives	33
6 2008–2012: Distribution Centrality	41
7 2013–2017: Harnessing Uncertainty	45
8 2018–2023: Measuring Uncertainty	50
Conclusions	58
References	60

Introduction

What you are about to read is the story of the attempt by physicists, economists, statisticians and mathematicians to explain how markets work based on concepts and tools taken from statistical mechanics. Shifting the focus of analysis from individuals to aggregates of individuals is the crux of this attempt.

It is well known that individual maximising behaviour – be it the utility or profit vector – is the basis for theoretical construction, enabling both partial and general equilibrium conditions to be designed. The market works because it is driven by maximising behaviour.

Shifting the perspective from the individual to the aggregate means that the end point of this interpretation is no longer to argue that an equilibrium exists, but to show that the macroscopic stability of a combination of variables – prices, incomes, rents and so on – is possible. If classical mechanics supported the construction of the economics of individuals, statistical mechanics proves useful to the economics of aggregates.

First a conceptual, subsequently a mathematical-statistical construction with numerous logical-empirical implications, the fascinating, lengthy history of the application of statistical mechanics in economics initially involved isolated scholars conducting niche research, and then became the subject of broader debate in the second half of the twentieth century, finally creating a new discipline – econophysics – at the beginning of this century. Running in parallel to mainstream economics, its conceptual assumptions are unlikely to bring the two disciplines together.

Econophysics is based on and has grown with statistical mechanics. Its seeds were sown by research carried out at the turn of the twentieth century, when statistical mechanics was becoming established and Vilfredo Pareto and Louis J. B. Bachelier independently published work on income distribution (Pareto, 1896–1897) and option pricing (Bachelier, 1900). Earlier still, sociophysics, the 'average man' of Adolphe Quetelet and the 'social physics' of Auguste Comte, prefigured econophysics, but it was the *kinetic theory of gases*, as set out by James Clerk Maxwell, Ludwig Eduard Boltzmann and subsequently Josiah Willard Gibbs, that led to *mechanical statistics*. The latter had been around for about a century when, in 1995, the physicist H. Eugene Stanley first introduced the term econophysics at a conference on socio-economics organised by physicists in Kolkata, India.

Economists greeted the probabilities and innovations provided by statistical physics cautiously, for many years clinging to classical mechanics. The reluctance persisted until a growing number of isolated researchers began to study broad *aggregates*, including monetary aggregates, the distribution of income and wealth and the prices of financial products. Markets were viewed as large ensembles (the term introduced by Gibbs) of agents and studied as entities in their own right, rather than on the basis of the behaviour of the individuals within them. Introducing his textbook on statistical mechanics, Sethna wrote: 'Statistical mechanics allows us to solve en masse many problems that are impossible to solve individually' (Sethna, 2021: 49). Anchoring economics in mechanical statistics enables problems to be tackled that economic individualism and microscopic analysis preclude.

The study of aggregates immediately required a form of representation that did not always coincide with a normal or Gaussian distribution. Other, often asymmetrical, distributions were introduced, to represent markets where mean and variance were unknown, based on the analogy between particles in a gaseous or liquid system and agents in a closed market. Energy exchanges between particles, as studied by kinetic theory, and the motion of molecules in a liquid system provided concepts that could be imported into economics and finance. And not only concepts but tools as well, taken from statistical mechanics and the study of particles, were applied to economic and financial phenomena.

The construction of economic and financial analysis from statistical mechanics was not merely a metaphorical exercise or a simple analogy from one discipline to another but involved a radical rethinking and reinterpretation of phenomena. Just as in the Maxwell–Boltzmann ideal gas model, particles in a closed system reach a point of thermal equilibrium by exchanging energy, so agents in a market reach a distribution of wealth and income by exchanging, which can take a variety of forms, ranging from normal (Gaussian) to more commonly skewed distributions. And the initial endowments are irrelevant.

Exchanges between agents, driven by talent, skill and information, are such that they lead to a probabilistic distribution with concentrations of wealth on the one hand and widespread income poverty or wealth on the other. From a statistical mechanics perspective, it is superfluous to interpret the factor driving exchange; what matters is describing and comparing the actual results. Unlike other approaches, statistical mechanics assumes that market mechanisms determine distribution based on the repetition of transactions.

The final distribution does not result from the initial inequality but is the product of exchanges between agents enriching one side and impoverishing the other. The probability of an agent retaining the same initial endowment after a series of exchanges or investments is very low, and the probability that the endowment changes is very high. This result is what most distinguishes the application of statistical mechanics to finance and economics.

Statistical mechanics may have taken almost a century to gain acceptance in economics, but it was a century rich in conceptual insights and theoretical innovations. Econophysics, and with it the study of complexity, took up the legacy of this long journey, becoming by the end of the twentieth century an independent field of economic and financial research, inspired by statistical mechanics.

A single thread links the theoretical innovations of the early twentieth century with the econophysics of the latter part of the century. The focus on aggregates – ultimately attention to large markets, the replacement of the deterministic by the probabilistic view, the acceptance of random behaviour and recognition that certain phenomena are only visible at the macroscopic level – becomes the constant feature of a research programme painstakingly taking shape until it becomes econophysics (Garibaldi & Scalas, 2010).

The programme was based not only on concepts but also on shared analytical tools. In particular, the treatment of non-Gaussian and heavy-tailed distributions in price series, income and wealth distributions and other social phenomena represents the approach associated with econophysics (Shubik & Smith, 2009: 10). The focus is on non-Gaussian distributions because they can probabilistically express the inequality of interactions between individuals. Indeed, heavy-tailed distributions allow for extreme and exceptional events, and this compels us to change the commonly accepted view of economics as a science of averages underlying economic equilibrium. As Benoît Mandelbrot (2009: 59) argues, it is precisely the assertion that the normal or Gaussian distribution prevails that gives economics the precision that brings it closer to classical physics. To admit that economic phenomena correspond to other skewed distributions, which admits randomness and reduced precision, is to enter the realm of economics and finance reinterpreted by statistical physics.

The emergence of a new, broad field of research is neither sudden nor unexpected. It is the result of insights, years of trial and error and often sporadic research with no follow-up. However, even if these efforts seemed fruitless at first, they have gradually contributed to the emergence of a new field of research, helping to define its objectives and boundaries and to establish its internal coherence. Part I of this Element is devoted to a century of initially fragmented, isolated and generally neglected research that slowly became a research programme in econophysics. This only proved apparent at the end of the twentieth century. The attention paid to the use of mechanical statistics in the 1930s was undoubtedly considered impromptu and extravagant. However, in a long-term perspective, the work has shown itself to embody courageous foresight.

The birth of a new scientific field is never deterministic. The sporadic reflections mentioned so far ultimately created a cultural context that was conducive to the emergence and recognition of the new discipline. Part II of our journey is devoted to the new field of econophysics, originating at the start of the millennium. Its history is as yet brief, only a quarter of a century, but its wealth of contents and ideas suggests that the discipline is developing fast. Econophysics is characterised by a scientific enthusiasm that has become contagious, leaving few indifferent to its future.

Part I A Long Road (1896–2000)

1 The Fundamentals

Statistical Mechanics and the Focus on Aggregates

The story begins at the turn of the twentieth century, when research by Maxwell and Boltzmann on the behaviour of gas molecules in a closed container coincided with the lengthy debate on probability, animating social and political spheres, where considerations of population and wealth distribution were familiar. Probability crossed over into the natural sciences, physics and social disciplines, stimulating a conceptual and methodological transformation known transversally as the probabilistic revolution (Krüger et al., 1990). In physics it led to the foundation of statistical mechanics (Ehrenfest & Ehrenfest, 1990) and elsewhere challenged the deterministic faith behind natural and social analysis, providing glimpses of new knowledge about the interaction of elements (whether particles or agents).

Two dates are symbolic of the transformation of physics: 1870, with the birth of statistical mechanics, a new theory or 'new kind of knowledge' in the words of James Clerk Maxwell (see Harman, 1998); and 1926, with the shift of attention to quantum mechanics, coinciding with Erwin Schrödinger's wave function and its probabilistic interpretation by Max Born (see Krüger, 1990). It was precisely in the 1920s that the emergence of these new branches of knowledge also 'contaminated' political economy.

The behaviour of particle aggregates studied according to the kinetic theory of gases, the central concern of the earliest applications of mechanical statistics, aroused the curiosity of some economists and statisticians who sought analogies with the behaviour of individuals in contexts where large numbers are present and able to carry out transactions – of any kind – with each other. Even in general terms, the market lent itself to such thinking, bringing kinetic theory into the vocabulary of economists and statisticians, who decided to pursue the analogy, however episodically. And this despite the fact that the world of physics in the 1920s had turned its attention away from particle aggregates towards quantum mechanics.

The meeting of the social and exact sciences was facilitated by the approach of the early probability theorists in relation to the study of gas particles. Maxwell, Boltzmann and Gibbs affirmed the existence of a correspondence between experimental data and probability distributions, without claiming that these distributions corresponded precisely with the state of the system. In its early years, the kinetic theory of gases recognised a degree of inaccuracy in determining the velocities or positions of the particles under study: the accurate macroscopic representation of the system coexisted with an approximate microscopic representation. This finding was taken up by the economists who sketched the first kinetic models of prices and incomes. Previously, liquids had suggested analogies with monetary liquidity (see Morgan, 2012: 172); now, gases came to be used not only metaphorically but also as conceptual tools to study economic phenomena.

The so-called marginalist revolution in economics was in its infancy when kinetic theory suggested studying ensembles rather than individual units. However, earlier classical and mercantilist thinking dealt with macro, not micro, quantities and variables. And it is precisely because income, wealth and money, that is, stocks and quantities, are relevant independently of their distribution among individuals that they were the first objects to be studied through the application of kinetic theory. This is an important point indicating that the application of statistical mechanics to economics, and later to finance, was never intended to spread over the whole of economics, but focused on the macroscopic analysis of large aggregates.

One idea in the kinetic theory of gases that economists liked was the notion of constructing a macroscopic representation on the basis of the binary transactions taking place between agents (as between particles), according to the principle of the conservation of wealth and energy. Although the number of gas molecules in a closed container is far larger than the number of agents in the social sphere, if collisions recurring in a state of stationarity with unchanged energy produce stability or order, the same was thought to be possible with financial, economic or social variables.

The shift of the (few) economists towards the macroscopic level, implicit in the analogy with statistical mechanics, was possible via a series of conceptual and methodological transformations during those years, in particular the spread of probabilities and their application to distribution curves. The economists who ventured into the terrain of statistical mechanics were among the first to advocate the use of probability in economics, although the probabilistic revolution did not occur until the 1930s (see Ménard, 1990; Morgan, 1990). As we shall see, probability distributions appeared in the study of the transition from micro- to macroeconomic conditions as early as the first years of the 1920s, shortly after Gibbs (1914) had demonstrated their relevance in the study of ensembles in thermal equilibrium.

The spread of probability influenced the use of important statistical concepts. As is well known, the great achievements of the statistical-probabilistic disciplines were obtained by assuming the principle of stochastic independence (and, conversely, dependence). Daniel Bernoulli, Pierre-Simon Laplace, Abraham de Moivre and Siméon-Denis Poisson made the principle of independence explicit, and it also features in the construction of Johann C. F. Gauss's theory of errors. The principle was partially abandoned at the beginning of the twentieth century, due to Max Planck and Andrei Markov, who rejected independence in favour of stochastic dependence in the development of quantum physics.

Stochastic independence is relevant to economics because it allows data to be aggregated without the risk of bias due to correlations between individual variables. But it is precisely the interpretation of emergent properties, the result of correlations between variables, that forces us to replace independence with stochastic dependence. On the other hand, it is difficult to imagine the outcome of interactions between individuals acting in a market without some form of correlation or mutual distortion. And not only that. The asymmetric outcome of the distribution, which must be regarded as a collective phenomenon, can also be explained by such interactions.

An ensemble of variables must be represented by a distribution, be it normal or Gaussian, derived from the law of errors, one of the main legacies of the eighteenth century, or an exponential, gamma or power-law distribution and so on. What matters is the ability to represent the order of the particles as economic variables (incomes, prices, yields), including all the phenomena that could influence them. This is how phenomena observed in nature, including extreme phenomena, are represented.

The initial imports from statistical mechanics transformed classical physics. Not so economics, finance or the social sciences, where the concepts introduced at the beginning of the century stabilised and gained strength until the end of the century, when econophysics emerged as a new field of research.

In econophysics texts, the events most often cited as foundational for the discipline are the publication of the income distribution curve by Pareto and the use of Brownian motion in the study of financial option prices by Bachelier. Although not explicitly linked to contemporary developments in statistical mechanics, the two ideas, albeit diverse, were part of a wave of conceptual transformations. Pareto published his distribution curves in the *Cours d'Économie Politique* in 1896–1897 (previewed in an article in 1896) (Pareto, 1896–1897);

Bachelier presented his thesis on financial speculation, *Théorie de la Spéculation*, which cited Brownian motion, in 1900 (Bachelier, 1900). In the history of ideas, the two theories had very different destinies: Pareto's income curve immediately aroused curiosity and debate, while Bachelier's thesis was not translated into English or republished until the 1960s, when it was rediscovered by Paul Samuelson.

Whatever the different publishing histories and reception of these two theories, econophysicists came to acknowledge them as fundamental to their discipline, essentially for two reasons. The first concerns the subject matter of both: the incomes received by an aggregate of individuals and the prices of a graded set of options exchanged by individuals, both being aggregates of variables. The fact that both the incomes received by a set of individuals and the prices of the options exchanged by individuals were regarded as random variables made it possible to adopt the approach of statistical mechanics and to represent these aggregates of variables probabilistically by means of distribution curves resulting from interactions between individuals. This will be the common thread running through all the attempts to apply statistical mechanics to economics and statistics in the twentieth century, right up to the creation of the discipline of econophysics.

Vilfredo Pareto's Stylised Fact

Pareto was sceptical about the analogy with the kinetic theory of gases, and paid little attention to statistical equilibrium until his late works, yet his income distribution curve is one of the pillars of econophysics. Known for its negative slope, its heavy tail at the bottom and the concentration of the highest incomes in the hands of the few, the Pareto curve is familiar to statisticians, physicists and economists, as well as to a wider audience of non-specialists.

Most often compared to Léon Walras as the founder of general economic equilibrium and the animator of the Lausanne School, Pareto, an engineer by training, was not only an economist whose optimality and other important insights are remembered in the history of the discipline but also a political scientist, best known for his theory of the circulation of elites, and the author of a massive treatise on sociology (Pareto, 1916).

Something similar to the circulation of elites can be found in his income distribution, since he does not exclude circulation in both directions, towards higher and lower incomes, although these movements are concentrated in the middle of the curve and the middle-income brackets. The distributions at the top and in the heavy tail, that is, the highest and lowest (and more widespread) incomes, respectively, are more stable.

The income (and wealth) curve is a 'stylised fact' and as such represents a kind of empirical exception in Pareto's thinking. Stylised fact or rule of thumb, he shows that the asymmetric distribution of income (and wealth) is repeated in countries and cities at different levels of development and over different time periods. Pareto presented his analysis first in an article in 1896 and then in *Cours* (Pareto, 1896–1897), where it immediately attracted international interest. The same interpretation of the income curve appears in later works (Pareto, 1906).

Interestingly, not all incomes are examined, but only those above the threshold (however low) of taxability. Lower incomes, often subsidised and with donations, are excluded because they lie outside the market and are not the result of commercial transactions.

Of Pareto's three versions of the income curve, he preferred the first because of greater coherence with the income data gathered. Given N, the number of income units above a certain income threshold, x, A is a positive scale parameter and α a parameter representing the slope of a curve expressed in terms of income frequencies. Pareto expresses the equation of the income curve as follows: $N = A/x^\alpha$ (1896–1897, §958). A logarithmic representation of the curve is also provided and is useful to understand the decreasing distribution of income.

The second version of the curve corresponds to: $N = A/(x+a)^\alpha$ (Pareto, 1896–1897: §961): a parameter a was added to restrict the range of incomes to above the survival threshold considered in the analysis. Clearly, increasing the constant a narrows the range of incomes considered, as if Pareto were primarily interested in studying the distribution of high incomes. The third equation (Pareto, 1896–1897: §958) approximates the income curve to a normal distribution by broadening the incomes, but was soon abandoned because of its discrepancy with the available data.

Pareto does not provide a version of the curve in terms of a probability distribution – with one exception at the end of the *Cours* (1896–1897: 416–419) – reiterating that the starting point can only be empirical. He concentrated instead on the logarithmic application. The slope of the curve depends on the much-debated value of the exponent α, which Pareto set at 1.5, considered to be sufficiently constant among different countries and historical periods. This value best fits the data observed by Pareto, giving us a universally valid rule of thumb. In the words of Mandelbrot (1960: 81), the negatively sloping logarithmic line represents the most significant Pareto law because the line refers to people with incomes only above the minimum level considered.

The normal distribution was rejected not for logical but for empirical reasons since the observed data would not lead to a normal distribution. The error curve would not be applicable because the observed distribution has a cause and cannot be attributed to chance, as error theory suggests.

Individuals, even in a number of heterogeneous groups (based on income), can be represented according to a hyperbolic distribution of individual qualities or abilities (talent). The curve would thus represent a statistical equilibrium determined by the heterogeneity of individuals. Circulation, similar to the circulation of elites proposed by Pareto in the political sphere, is not excluded, but does not alter the complex configuration precisely because of the concentration in the middle range of incomes and of the curve.

The extremes – the highest and lowest incomes – remain stable, while shifts occur in the middle range of the income distribution. The negative slope of the curve is therefore solely due to the asymmetric distribution of individual talents. Heterogeneity forced Pareto to reject the assumptions of equiprobability: agents are not equiprobable in terms of income possibilities, nor does the imposition of an equal distribution help. Indeed, 'human nature' as the cause of the distribution of wealth (Pareto, 1896–1897: §957) means that what Pareto calls the economic organism, that is, the institutional structure, plays no role. The distribution of wealth, and hence of income, is the result of (family, market, price-mediated) transactions between individuals.

This is confirmed by a clear multifractal view of income distribution, which can be seen when he writes that when one draws the distribution lines for countries of different sizes, 'it looks as if one were drawing a large number of crystals of the same chemical substance. There are large crystals, medium crystals and small crystals, but they all have the same shape' (Pareto, 1896–1897: §958). This is a mercantile, non-institutional view of income distribution.

Pareto did not consider kinetic theory and probability when formulating his income theory, but the conclusions on the role of trade and markets are close to those adopted subsequently by econophysics. The distinction between income groups set out in the section added to the *Cours* is used in the *Treatise* to focus on a society organised into social groups, and this led Pareto to consider a possible analogy with kinetic theory, which is probabilistic by definition. Pareto introduced the analogy with statistical equilibrium from the kinetic theory of gases (1916: §2074) by considering how the actions of individuals compensate each other, resulting in oscillating states leading to a general equilibrium and a stable trend.

The analogy with gas theory is based on the observation that society comprises units (molecules) that are more heterogeneous than those that make up the economy (Pareto,1916: §2079), also recognising the advantages of forming groups of individuals with similar incomes, interests and sentiments (Pareto, 1922: §1124). By comparing the group to a centre of energy, Pareto seems to refer to the future quantum theory.

Bachelier's Random Walk

Identifying a criterion, if not a law, for the context-independent pricing of shares, Bachelier's *Théorie de la Spéculation* (1900) is rightly regarded as a founding text of financial economics and econophysics. The causality characterising the formation of option prices in Bachelier's financial market, seemingly far removed from talent and other factors underlying income distribution, actually shares with Pareto the naturalness of the mechanism that would regulate the market. The main difference lies in the distribution of the variables, which is almost hyperbolic in the case of Pareto's income and Gaussian in the case of Bachelier's prices. The small option price movements observed over a short period are independent of the previous and current prices of the financial asset in question and are independent of the price movements of other options (Brownian motion). Precisely because price fluctuations are case dependent and stochastically independent, and taking into account the central limit theorem, they can be traced back to an error curve with a Gaussian distribution. The differences lie in the conceptualisation of motion and, above all, in the presence of short, stochastically independent movements.

Although the end point is a normal distribution, Bachelier profoundly innovated the approach to financial markets. The conceptual scheme required by the application of the Brownian motion is very different from that of classical mechanics or dynamics. The particle under examination has a motion expressed not in differential but in probabilistic terms. By analogy, the price of an option has a probability distribution. The problem, therefore, is to identify the type of distribution that characterises a memoryless particle driven by a fluctuating force (i.e., white noise, or an osmotic force).

The equation representing a diffusion process expresses the probability, p, that the option is quoted x' at time t_1 and that the probability of price x is quoted at time $t_1 + \Delta t$ as follows: $p(x, t + \Delta t) = \frac{1}{2\pi k \sqrt{t}} exp\left[-\frac{x^2}{4\pi k^2 t}\right]$ (Bachelier, 1900: 137), where $k = \frac{1}{2\pi H}$ (with H = constant) is the positive mathematical expectation of x at $t = 1$, here taken as a constant. Mathematical expectations of prices (Bachelier, 1900: 147), all of which depend on the square root of time, are statistically indistinguishable after a few steps, so it can be said that each price behaves like the others. The same result was clearly established by Einstein in 1905, although Einstein was unaware of Bachelier when he pointed out to scientists trying to measure the velocity of a microscopic particle that the average velocity in an interval t is inversely proportional to $\sqrt{t}$.

Later, Norbert Wiener fully defined Brownian motion as a two-dimensional process taking into account the position and velocity of the particle (Wiener, 1921; Genthon, 2020). Ideally, if the particle is moved by a fluctuating force, it assumes values entirely irrespective of its past history. Brownian motion represented in this way can therefore be considered Markovian. And Markovian, independent of past values, are the prices of Bachelier's options. Equally, if we look not at the single motion of a particle but at a series of motions, we obtain a random walk where the independence of each step is balanced by the sum of the previous steps to arrive at the current position.

In *The Random Character of Stock Market Prices* (1964), a volume that contains the first English translation of Bachelier's *Théorie de la Spéculation* (*Theory of Speculation*), Paul Cootner (1964) points out that the density function assumed by Bachelier includes its continuous differentiation with respect to t, that it is possible to find prime and partial derivatives with respect to prices, and that mean and variance are finite. Thus, in Bachelier's world of option prices, infinitely divisible – starting with Gaussian – distributions are considered.

In the same 1964 volume, Matthew F. M. Osborne points out that Brownian motion does not necessarily imply the absence of an underlying rational structure. While not denying the premise that the most likely value of the expected change in the logarithm of the price of a randomly chosen common stock at a random time is zero, Osborne argues that, under certain conditions and at certain times, it is possible to find a sample of stocks for which the expected change is slightly different from zero. Osborne's conclusion that the stock market is a gigantic decision-making phenomenon (Osborne, 1964: 295), to which scale invariance can be applied, foreshadows the macroscopic approach of econophysics.

The random variables left over from Bachelier's model express the joint risk of buying and selling shares. Because of their independence and their Gaussian shape, these variables make it possible, for a given time horizon t, to calculate a return as the result of many independent shocks which, according to the central limit theorem, give rise to a Gaussian distribution of returns. The next step is to transform a discontinuous probability into a continuous and therefore differentiable distribution, an operation that Bachelier was unable to carry out because he did not have the mathematical tools subsequently developed by Andrej N. Kolmogorov in 1931. However, the attempt to transform apparently random price movements into a normal distribution was clear.

The adoption of the Gaussian distribution was a hallmark of theoretical research in finance. It was widely used because of the simplifications it allows – such as in the Black–Scholes stock price calculation – which are more applicable to finance than to economics.

However, Brownian motion has another characteristic placing Bachelier's theory at the origin of econophysics. Measuring single particle properties allows these properties to be extended to several particles to determine a diffusion coefficient expressing volatility. In statistical physics, the average statistical properties of a single particle are equivalent to the statistical properties of an ensemble of particles (see Schweitzer, 2003: 40–41). As Mandelbrot (2009) has pointed out, the main point of applying Brownian motion to option pricing is that price increases are statistically independent and Gaussian, implying that the price itself is a continuous function of time with a stochastic component describing random fluctuations.

Lévy Flights

In the 1920s and 1930s, the mathematician Paul Lévy (1925, 1937–1954, 1948–1965) investigated a class of random functions now called Lévy processes, which are a generalisation of Brownian motion characterised by steps that are stationary, statistically self-sufficient and stably distributed. However, the length of the steps differs from Brownian motion, which is notoriously short. This is the case of Lévy flights, which can be much longer, actually creating real discontinuities. Although there is no evidence that Lévy was familiar with Pareto's insights, Lévy's flights bring Brownian motion closer to Pareto's heavy tails, where the variance is not finite but infinite.

Later, in a 1960 article, 'The Pareto-Lévy law and the distribution of income', Mandelbrot links Pareto to Lévy in an effort to convince his readers of the usefulness of stable non-Gaussian distributions. Clearly, stability depends on the heavy-tailed portion, where the link to Lévy is evident. So Lévy can be used to add stability to the Pareto distribution.

Micro More Than Macro Insights: Quantum Mechanics

Statistical mechanics undoubtedly provides the main foundation of econophysics: concepts such as particle interactions, variations in velocity and heat transfer are central to the kinetic theory of gases, which has been adopted and adapted in economics and finance. By contrast, quantum mechanics – although often cited in modern econophysics – plays a less clearly defined role. Certainly, quantum mechanics provides a more thorough analysis of uncertainty in models based on statistical mechanics, bringing the analysis back to molecules (agents). In any case, the frequency with which it appears in econophysics papers is surprising. The elements of early quantum mechanics that are useful for understanding recent developments in econophysics are detailed in the following paragraphs.

With contributions from Max Planck, Niels H. D. Bohr, Werner K. Heisenberg, Erwin R. J. A. Schrödinger and others, quantum mechanics developed alongside statistical mechanics, introducing two essential elements into the origins of econophysics. The first concerned the nature of energy, no longer regarded as a continuous quantity that can be expressed statistically by the particles comprising the system being analysed. Energy became discrete quantities assigned to the analysed units on the basis of a probabilistic measurement. Although discrete, as a stochastic quantity (Mirowski, 1989: 86) energy could not be measured with absolute precision. In fact, the concept of a wave function was used to describe the probability of finding a particle or quantity of energy in a particular state.

The second element concerned stochastic independence, which became dependence: molecules (agents) cannot choose their cell (income) without taking into account what happens to other molecules (agents). Thus, among other things, *wavelength functions* replaced collisions between particles and *entanglement* (connections) replaced interactions. Essentially, while gas particles are distinguishable from each other and thus metaphorically equated with agents, quanta, as granules of energy, are not distinguishable from each other (Costantini, 2004: 193). Probability is still central. The challenge that quantum mechanics poses to economics and finance seems to involve a re-conceptualisation of the market, characterised no longer by certain but by probable relationships.

In quantum mechanics, the search for the causes of a phenomenon is no longer crucial, because if no cause is apparent, it is simply postulated that there is no cause. This means that the laws of physics are indeterministic and can only be expressed in terms of probabilities (Jaynes, 2003: 328). Unlike in statistical mechanics, where the causes of a phenomenon may be identified intuitively, in quantum mechanics ignorance of causes is translated into probabilities or, rather, probabilities overcome the problem of causes by elevating chance to a central role.

When moving from statistical to quantum mechanics, the analysis of aggregates or ensembles becomes more complex. This increased complexity stems from Heisenberg's uncertainty principle: because the position and momentum of a quantum system cannot be determined simultaneously, such a system cannot be represented as a point in phase space. Furthermore, probability densities can take on different configurations and moments, so a second level of probability is required to account for the fact that the system can have a variety of quantum states, that is, positions, velocities, directions and other properties. This explains why ensembles in quantum mechanics are called mixed states, a kind of statistical mixture of different quantum states. Mixed states are immersed in uncertainty and are characterised by decisions made with incomplete information. To understand this characteristic of quantum mechanics, the state of an ensemble with properties corresponds to the set of values these properties take. One such property could be the list of molecules that make up the ensemble, giving the microscopic state of the ensemble. Examining this ensemble in isolation, we can measure and observe it in its deterministic evolution, as in kinetic theory. Unlike in classical mechanics, quantum states can overlap.

When we examine a quantum state, correlations between different parts of a quantum system become observable. This phenomenon is known as entanglement. In mixed states, however, a given subsystem or particle may belong to several quantum states simultaneously. As a result, the entanglement between two states gives rise to intrinsic uncertainties that are characteristic of the states themselves, rather than reflecting limitations in our knowledge of them. While the mixing of different states is an uncommon feature of classical mechanics, the entanglement of parts of states is specific to quantum mechanics. In a debtor–creditor relationship, a change in the state of one party immediately affects the other. Debt, like the price of an option, is a number, and the relationship of that number to a commodity. If in statistical mechanics a molecule can be compared to an agent, in quantum mechanics the analogue of the particle is a number describing a relationship. Reality becomes a numerical or mathematical reality, or rather a reality described by mathematically calculated probability amplitudes. But it is precisely the emphasis on numbers, which express discrete amounts of energy (quanta), that makes quantum mechanics more suitable for microscopic than for macroscopic analysis.

2 Early Attempts to Use Statistical Mechanics in Economics

Dealing with 'Living Energy'

The curve put forward by Pareto immediately led Italian mathematicians, statisticians and economists to transform the asymmetric Pareto distribution into a probability distribution. In particular, in the 1920s, the mathematician Francesco P. Cantelli used the second version of Pareto's equation to show that it could be expressed according to a frequentist interpretation (see Tusset, 2018). In *Sulla deduzione di legge di frequenza da considerazioni di probabilità* (*On the Deduction of Frequency Law from Probability Considerations*) in 1921, Cantelli compared the distribution of income to the distribution of velocities of gas molecules (1921: 89), the first explicit comparison of economic analysis to statistical mechanics, after the indirect analogy in Bachelier's theory of speculation. The comparison was with a column of gas molecules in a closed container with total energy (kinetic and potential) a given. However, moving to the economic sphere, the problem arises of how to identify a quantity, functioning as a constant, that corresponds to the energy associated with the volume of gas.

This is the problem of André-Marie Ampère's *vis viva*, which becomes *living energy* with Guido Castelnuovo, a mathematician (1919). In a 1921 article, Cantelli considers the total utility derived from disposable income as a given, while the utility of individual agents varies as a result of exchanges. Utility is therefore like energy circulating in the system. Given the constraint adopted, Cantelli shows that the most likely distribution of income (source of utility) corresponds to the Pareto income equation $N = A/(x+a)^\alpha$. However, Cantelli does not identify the factors leading to this income distribution other than exchange (the market) itself, and ends up seeing chance as the determining factor. The attainment of an income, x, depends on a complicated interweaving of causes (activity, skill, competition, character of the individual, constitution, etc.), so that it seems to depend on chance (Cantelli, 1921: 90). Although criticised (e.g. because measuring the total utility of income did not seem possible), Cantelli's attempt was used in research on the probabilistic distribution of income in Italy and elsewhere between the two world wars.

Cantelli returned to the subject in 1929, assuming that the stock to be distributed was the number of working hours and that workers could choose how much to work, thereby determining their income. The stability of the distribution was guaranteed by the fact that wages were ultimately determined by the workers themselves. In this way, Cantelli sought to overcome the abstract nature of utility, replacing it with the total stock of working hours which corresponded to the stock of income. Recently, drawing on Cantelli's 1929 article, Jess Benhabib and Alberto Bisin (2018: 1264, footnote 9) have argued that the relevant variable to consider is neither utility nor hours worked but, rather, total talent, which they regard as being distributed according to a multinomial probability across equiprobable income groups. In Cantelli's thinking, the choice of hours was a simplified representation of the exchange mechanisms leading to the Pareto distribution.

Cantelli prompted the reflections of the economist and statistician Felice Vinci, who reformulated the second Pareto equation in terms of the density of the distribution curve (Vinci, 1921: 368). The probability of falling into an income segment, Vinci wrote, depended on two factors: personal qualities (talent) and numerous other definable institutional elements. Talent, useful for the acquisition of income, appeared to be concentrated in the higher income population. Institutional factors appeared as barriers to entry increasing with income. Translated into parameters, these factors enabled Vinci (1921, 1924) to approximate an exponential distribution expressed by a Pearson-type V curve, otherwise known as an inverse gamma distribution, characterised by the presence of a heavy tail.

But Vinci's conclusion was clear: the distribution of income depends on such a complex of causes that it seems to rely on chance (1921: 369). Chance here is not an imponderable but, rather, the outcome of many – perhaps an excess of – random and chaotic factors. A similar conclusion can be found in the work of Dunkan K. Foley, who argues that the statistical equilibrium underlying income distribution is a chaotic process that tends to explore all possible patterns of income transactions (Foley, 2003: 102).

Another important contribution of the time was provided by the mathematician Luigi Amoroso (1925). Based on the second Pareto equation revisited by Cantelli and Vinci's inverse gamma function, he focused on the parameterisation needed to include what Pareto had excluded, that is, lower income brackets. The result is a unimodal, rather than a (Pareto) zero-modal, curve. This gives a gamma distribution that can be written as the following density function: $f(x) = Ce^{-y(x-x_0)^{\frac{1}{s}}}(x-x_0)^{\frac{y-s}{s}}$, where $f(x)$ is the number of agents with an income ranging between x and $x_0 + dx$, and $x_0 < x < \infty$; a is a positive integer; x_0 is a positive or nil integer; y is a positive integer; and s is a positive integer such as $p + s > 0$. The Amoroso curve, still used today, is a generalisation of the special case of the Pareto curve. If $p = 1$, Amoroso's distribution is the same as Pareto's, with zero-modal characteristics. As the value of p increases to 2, 3, 4, ..., the peak makes its appearance, and the distribution takes on the well-known spinning top shape. According to the value and sign of the parameters, the gamma distribution lies between a normal and a Pareto distribution.

Remembered today in econophysics for his gamma distribution, Amoroso also applied kinetic gas theory to monetary aggregates. In 1924, he published a short, little-known article, 'La cinematica in un mercato chiuso' ('Kinematics in a closed market'), which presented a monetary model he called 'kinetic' (Amoroso, 1924: 142), based on the familiar exchange equation $MV = PQ$. Amoroso argued that the equation of exchange is formally identical to the characteristic equation of gases, provided that the following correspondences hold: the quantity of money in circulation (M) corresponds to absolute temperature; the volume of exchange (Q) to the volume of the gas; the price level (P) to gas pressure; and the velocity of circulation of money (V) to the universal (Boltzmann) constant (Amoroso, 1924: 144). The price level, the gas pressure, is the critical variable that must be controlled by the other variables: money in circulation (by reduction) and the volume of transactions (by expansion).

Amoroso confines himself to this analogy without further elaboration. It was the first time an analogy had been drawn between stocks of money and gaseous quantities.

Amoroso's variable velocity of circulation of money was taken up in 1932 in an article written in Hungarian by Andrew Pikler and translated as 'A short groundwork of a kinetic theory of money'. Pikler interpreted the equation of exchange by analogy with the kinetic theory of gases, hence based on a plurality of stocks of money, each characterised by its own velocity of circulation (see Petracca, 2019). The analogy with molecules, each with its own velocity, is obvious. As Enrico Petracca notes, the article was reviewed in Italy (Del Vecchio) and cited in France (Moret). Pikler subsequently (1951) extended the analogy between the theory of money and kinetic theory, adding elements of quantum mechanics.

Interpreting the various monetary stocks – M_1, M_2, M_3 and so on – discussed by Amoroso and Pikler as monetary budgets helps to clarify the kinetic interpretation of household budgets proposed by Johannes Lisman in 1949 in *Econometrics, Statistics and Thermodynamics*. In this case, gas budgets were associated with 'closed' postage checks in the transfer system. Exchanges were equated with collisions, and postal deposits with collisions with the container walls. Lisman is interesting for two reasons. First, because he expressed total energy as the sum of the deposits used for cheques – that is, by equating the (postal) money stock with energy – whereas in physics energy is defined as a quadratic function of particle velocities, a feature that has no counterpart in the definition of money. Second, he shifted to a macro-analysis of the money stock, following Pikler (quoted explicitly), and applied Boltzmann's theorem H to show the link between the micro-analysis of postal cheques and the macro-analysis. Lisman ended up ruling out the analogy due to the impossibility of expressing postal cheque transactions in terms of probability distributions. While collisions between particles are reversible, there is no such reversibility in financial exchanges: we can reverse exchange transactions, but not at an unchanged price (Lisman, 1949: 88).

The analogy between thermodynamic and monetary systems was also explored by Meghnad Saha, an Indian nuclear physicist whose textbook *Treatise on Heat* (1931), co-authored with Biswambhar Nath Srivastava, suggested that students apply kinetic theory to the market in order to explain the asymmetric distribution of income and wealth (see Chakrabarti, 2018). The money market seems to fit the analogy because traders can neither create nor destroy money, which is conserved, analogous to kinetic energy in a closed gas system.

In the 1940s and 1950s the attempt to import statistical mechanics (kinetic gas theory) into economics was complemented by quantum mechanics. In 1943, Harro Bernardelli, an Austrian economist and refugee in Rangoon (Myanmar), argued for the substantial stability of Pareto's asymmetric income distribution in an article, 'The stability of income distribution', published in *Sankhyā: The Indian Journal of Statistics*. Bernardelli turned to quantum mechanics to study the process of transition to a stable equilibrium, borrowing the expansion theorem from Paul Dirac (1935). By employing Hamiltonian functions – which represent the total energy of a system and reintroduce irreversibility – Bernardelli sought to understand how initial conditions shape outcomes. The remaining challenge is to justify the emergence of a skewed distribution given a fixed total amount of wealth or income, which in this framework corresponds to total energy. To this end, the system is decomposed into income groups, treated as eigenstates, whose interactions are analysed using concepts drawn from quantum theory,

The probability of moving between income groups depends on the educational, cultural and institutional factors discussed earlier, which tend to operate slowly and therefore do not lead to rapid changes in the overall income distribution. Bernardelli allowed for movement between groups, an exchange of energy, but in such a way that the composition of and within groups remains stable, so that, as he stated in 1943, each income group reproduces in miniature the original composition of the whole society (Bernardelli, 1943: 357). He concluded that the rate of change in income is proportional to the deviation of that income from the equilibrium represented by the final distribution, which is by definition stable. Energy, however, only changes form, thus does not bring about real social change.

Some of Bernardelli's insights were developed in depth in David Champernowne's *A Model of Income Distribution* (1953), which uses an economic model to argue that the forces that determine the distribution of income in any community are so varied and complex, and interact and fluctuate so constantly, that any theoretical model must be either unrealistically simplified or hopelessly complicated (1953: 319). Hence his construction of the Pareto curve as an asymptotic curve at both the top and the bottom, a trend that leaves open the possibility of random changes. This conclusion led him to advise caution when predicting the effects of income policies (Champernowne, 1953: 351), as Pareto had done many years before (Pareto, 1906: 204).

Maria Castellani, an Italian mathematician, student of Cantelli and assistant to Castelnuovo before emigrating to the United States in the 1940s, published an article in 1950 entitled 'On multinomial distributions with limited freedom: A stochastic genesis of Pareto's and Pearson's curves', in which she moved from kinetic to quantum approaches. She called the quantum unit an 'energy interval' corresponding to an income group.

Castellani (1950) explained that each energy interval or income group was characterised by two independent forces, both functions of time. The two forces could vary, but the sum of the different energy intervals always yielded a constant, corresponding to a state of conservation of energy. Castellani did not describe the nature of the two forces that explain the Pareto or Pearson distributions. But individual talent, a single force in the case of Pareto, and talent plus institutions in the case of Pearson, perfectly represent the two independent forces. The distribution of energy between the two factors is uncertain and varies as a function of distance from the starting point, while the total remains constant.

As this brief and incomplete review shows, a number of elements recur in these models, all of which aim for a macroscopic or macroeconomic representation of phenomena. In particular, the principle of energy conservation recurs, accompanied by the search for a similar economic principle, the identification of which seems relevant because it is a constraint. Once the factor assumed as a constant is identified, the relevance of Pareto's second equation is verified in order to interpret the distribution. The constant treated as a constraint does not account for the distributional inequality that emerges from interactions among multiple factors, a process sometimes summarised by the term 'chance' (Cantelli, 1921; Vinci, 1921).

Majorana

The first phase of the application of mechanical statistics to economics and finance cannot be concluded without mentioning what an eminent physicist wrote on the subject of the encounter between the natural and social sciences. Ettore Majorana, a renowned physicist, wrote an essay in the 1930s entitled 'Il valore delle leggi statistiche nella fisica e nelle scienze sociali' ('The value of statistical laws in physics and in the social sciences'), published in *Scientia* in 1942 (translated into English only in 2006 – see Bassani and the Council of the Italian Physical Society (CIPS), 2006) after the disappearance of Majorana himself.

Majorana joins with Kolmogorov in the probabilistic revolution by identifying the statistical field – and probability – as the area where the natural and social sciences could converge on common methods and approaches. However, he was addressing his fellow physicists rather than social scientists, emphasising the lack of objectivity in phenomena and asserting the statistical nature of elementary processes (Bassani and the CIPS, 2006: 250).

Majorana argued that the introduction of a new type of statistical law in physics – or, more generally, of probabilistic laws often embedded in statistical ones – would require physicists to reconsider the foundations of the analogy with social statistical laws established earlier. The statistical character of social laws, which derives from the way in which the conditions of phenomena are defined, allows an innumerable range of concrete possibilities and probabilities to be considered as the core of the analogy between physical events and social facts (Bassani and the CIPS, 2006: 258). Although Majorana's position was forward-looking, it remained a minority view, grounded in the belief that the natural and social sciences could speak a common language, identified by him as the language of statistics, in which probability plays a fundamental role.

3 A New Discipline on the Way

Attempts to introduce elements of statistical mechanics into economic analysis in the first half of the twentieth century appeared to be rather isolated, the result of mostly individual interest, with almost no impact on the economic debate. The Pareto income distribution itself was set aside, except partially in Italy, where it continued to prompt interest and debate. Only in the second half of the century did the application of statistical mechanics to economics arouse the interest of economists and beyond, with the extension of the Pareto curve to areas other than income/wealth and the rediscovery of Bachelier's ideas. Intriguingly, Pareto and Bachelier seem to meet in the application of statistical mechanics to economics.

Random Economies

Interest in 'random economies with many interactive agents', to quote an article by Hans Föllmer from 1974, became widespread in the mid 1960s, especially among economists. Föllmer, a mathematician, first introduced the Ising model, based on ferromagnetic spin pairs, allowing the social interactions of economic agents to be modelled in relation to their preferences in a context of interdependence (Föllmer, 1974). He showed that in the presence of even short-ranging interactions, microeconomic characteristics can no longer determine the macroeconomic phase (see Chen & Li, 2012). Hence, interest turned to agents whose preferences and endowments are random, and the probabilities governing this randomness are determined by the environment, be it a market for real goods or financial products. Returning to Pareto's skewed distribution, we are in the middle of the curve, not on the heavy tails, where agents interact, determine and actually swap positions. In this part of the distribution, Brownian motion can be applied.

The approach is well represented in a collection of essays published in 1964 by Paul Cootner, *The Random Character of Stock Market Prices*, which included an English version of Bachelier's thesis under the title *Theory of Speculation*. Following Bachelier, the aim was to analyse the pricing of financial assets or, better still, to find a theory enabling predictions to be made about the return on investment in shares.

Despite mathematical improvements, Bachelier's view that a rational interpretation of option and stock prices can be constructed from random behaviour was maintained, after eliminating some limitations in Bachelier's analysis, the most important, from an economic point of view, being negative stock prices.

The assumptions introduced correspond to the standard economic interpretation of Brownian motion: prices are memoryless and mutually independent, and both their mean and their variance are finite. Extreme events are therefore excluded. A 'random walk' is assumed, which explains the movement of stock prices by their similarity to a series of random factors. The principle of stochastic independence and the absence of direct interaction between particles/agents complete a theoretical construction aimed at arguing the independence of an option price from other prices, a prerequisite for the set of prices to determine a normal distribution. This assumption differs from the interaction-based mechanism at the origin of the skewed distribution mentioned earlier.

For the economists who contributed to the book, an important theoretical corollary was undoubtedly the non-relationship of financial asset prices to past prices. The idea is of a market in which past prices play no role. This aspect, determined by analogy with Brownian motion, leads to an almost atemporal representation of the economic process, which is obviously an important step because atemporality does not arise from the difficulty of constructing a dynamic theory but, rather, is assumed as a fundamental aspect of price theory. Later, it became clear that the assumption of independent prices conflicted with expectations of price volatilities based on past volatilities.

In terms of distribution, the comparison was between the normal distributions with equally distributed left and right errors resulting from the application of Brownian motion to stock prices, and the Paretian distribution with heavy-tailed peaks. The question that remained open, then, was not the existence of random economies but the formation of prices in random economies: in a normal distribution, the central limit theorem allows prices to be independent after all. This is not so in a skewed distribution with heavy, potentially asymmetric tails, accompanied by peaks and extremes.

Mandelbrot and the Paretian Universe

It is this market, with its unique peaks and events, that Mandelbrot examines with an analytically rich and complex theory of incomes, prices and fractals, only hinted at here. What is interesting for our purposes is Mandelbrot's methodological approach: he tries to show that the analogy with statistical physics must not be abandoned if the weaknesses that plague existing theories are to be avoided. The way to do this, he argues, is not to seek the economic equivalent of statistical thermodynamics but to generalise the statistical methods of thermodynamics to the economic concept of income (Mandelbrot, 1960: 85). However, to better understand Mandelbrot's view of statistical physics, it is worth recalling that he considered Pareto's statistical law, which did not originate in physics, as central to both economics and physics (Mandelbrot, 1963a: 421). Mandelbrot suggested 'imitating' the principles of physics to interpret economic phenomena (1963a: 426). Hence, the economic variables did not need to be compressed into a framework of statistical thermodynamics; rather, the statistical methods of thermodynamics needed to be generalised to cover economic concepts such as income.

Mandelbrot's methodological position had an empirical origin. The data show that the Pareto income curve declines much more slowly than a normal physical law, with the consequence that traditional interpretations based on Bernoulli or Weber–Fechner can be applied to high and middle incomes but not to the heavy tail (Mandelbrot, 1960). Focusing on this, Mandelbrot explains the even extreme phenomena that can occur as a consequence of random interaction, starting from Pareto reinterpreted through Lévy.

In Mandelbrot's thinking, the two fields at the origin of econophysics – income distribution and Brownian motion in finance – converge into a single field of research that could be called Paretian process analysis. Process, because the Paretian tail characterises not only incomes and prices but also the distribution of firms by size and cities by size. And because the process is interpreted in its various domains on the basis of microfoundations, Mandelbrot refers to this method as 'invariant laws' (1963a: 423), a term he borrowed from physics and adapted for use in economics. Invariance refers mainly to the aggregation of variables such as income or firms of different sizes, which Mandelbrot regards as possible even where the variables to be aggregated are non-Gaussian. However, in the presence of Gaussian distributions, random variables are taken into account and not excluded.

Mandelbrot points out that the family of distributions identified by Paul Lévy in the 1920s (see Lévy, 1948–1965), which appear to be stable even when adding random variables is taken into account, includes non-Gaussian distributions (Mandelbrot, 1960: 86). These confirm the 'weak Pareto law' (see the first Pareto equation earlier), $0 < \alpha < 2$, characterised by a heavy tail, demonstrating that extreme events, however rare, follow a certain law and are significant. In particular, Mandelbrot defined 'Pareto–Lévy distributions' as 'positive', stable distributions with $1 < \alpha < 2$ (1960: 87). When $\alpha \geq 2$, the curve approaches a Gaussian distribution (Mandelbrot, 1963c). Since the stability of the distribution is ensured by finite values of the first two moments, mean and variance, one consequence of $1 < \alpha < 2$ is that the second moment becomes infinite, while the first is finite. The focus is on the length of the tail, rather than the extreme skewness of the curve, because this is the most significant aspect of Pareto's law, or the Paretian process, to use his words (Mandelbrot, 1963a: 422). According to Mandelbrot, an increase in the number of random variables leads to an extension of the heavy tail. The idea is to start the analysis with the highest incomes and then gradually add the lowest incomes distributed in the heavy tail.

What led Mandelbrot to comment on the Brownian motion introduced by Bachelier was again an empirical finding. Prices tend to have peaks that can scarcely be expressed in the normal distribution assumed by Brownian motion. The tails of the distributions of price changes are so extraordinarily long that the variance of the samples is typically erratic (Mandelbrot, 1963b: 394–395). The market emerging from Mandelbrot's analysis has an instability not encountered in Cootner or in other economists. Consequently, the Brownian motion of Bachelier becomes a special case of the application of Pareto–Lévy processes. Mandelbrot (1960) explicitly referred to the Pareto distribution as an alternative to the Gaussian distribution of Brownian motion, which, in the version of Pareto himself, with α parameter below 2, has variance that can be infinite.

With Mandelbrot, the thinking of Pareto and Bachelier comes together in the application of Lévy's processes, raising the problem of infinite variance that is a challenge for the analysis of financial markets. After some repetition, the small random movements of variables (Brownian motion) predict a martingale environment, that is, expectations reflect current values. However, in the presence of heavy tails, where the frequencies of neighbouring values become significant, Lévy flights can develop, that is, large deviations from the mean that are essentially unpredictable and whose frequency (periodic crises) can be loosely assumed.

Despite resistance from some economists, heavy tails entered the toolkit of the discipline, until new empirical research appeared to demonstrate that the distributions of returns in financial markets tend to be Gaussian on time scales of over one month (Sornette, 2014). In the final decades of the twentieth century, research was moving back towards normal distributions. Nonetheless, with regard to the introduction of mechanical statistics into economics, Mandelbrot showed that the skewed distribution resulting from the interaction of agents (the market) can lead to peaks and crises, that is, extreme events.

Mandelbrot built on Pareto's insights not only by introducing the scaling properties of physical, economic and social phenomena (such as coastlines, firms and cities) but above all by interpreting the relationships among Gaussian, log-normal and power-law distributions. In so doing, he highlighted both their potential and their limitations, extending their relevance beyond their traditional uses in finance, economics and physics (see Mirowski, 1990). To fully understand their application, randomness is considered to be binary – either non-random or random – but gradual – light, slow and wild. Markets should be studied from the heavy tails.

Steindl's Random Processes

In the early 1960s, the Austrian economist Josef Steindl was similarly interested in tails, albeit not as heavy as in Mandelbrot. Steindl's original contribution, inspired by Pareto, consisted in the study of firm size in relation to growth.

He classified companies in different sectors and countries according to their business and number of employees. The result is a skewed distribution with a slope coefficient (the Pareto α) between 1.5 and 2. According to Steindl, the long tail of the Pareto distribution represents companies – defined by assets and number of employees, not by number of manufacturing plants – with sizes that do not cluster around an average value. A log-normal distribution, such as Robert Gibrat's (1931), would fit well in the middle, excluding the extremes. However, while allowing for heavy tails with extreme values, Steindl makes it clear that the variance of the random variables under consideration is not infinite. Steindl (1965: 19) seems to be telling us that economists allow for random but finite variables. Beyond the technical aspects, what is significant here is the meaning to be attached to the extreme value.

Steindl's idea can be seen as an attempt to explain the random process leading to Pareto's asymmetric income distribution from the size of profits (part of the income distribution) via the size of firms. Although Steindl considers the Pareto distribution to be the most realistic for the representation of the transformations (birth/death) characterising firms, he does not neglect the growth processes represented by log-normal distributions, such as those of Robert Gibrat and Jacobus Kapteyn. He refers to the law of proportional effects, originating with Gibrat (1931), and, more interestingly, to the random walk (and Brownian movement) as an analogy to firms, which therefore move towards a log-normal and, in particular, stable distribution (Steindl, 1965: 31). The process has a time dimension, not too long, because the passage of time increases the variance of the Brownian motion.

Steindl reinterprets Pareto's α as the outcome of opposing growth rates: the rate of birth and death of firms, the rate of appearance and disappearance of wealth holders. The equilibrium between opposing forces determines the Pareto coefficient, as Pareto himself had noted in the *Treatise on General Sociology*

(1916: §2074), where he states that the oscillating states of individuals can generate a general equilibrium.

The Law of Chaos

Economics and statistical mechanics meet again in *Laws of Chaos: A Probability Approach to Political Economy*, published by Emmanuel Farjoun and Moshé Machover in 1983. Statistical mechanics is taken as a paradigm providing a probabilistic reinterpretation of the Marxian view of economics, starting with the definition of profit as a random variable. The application to production of the relationship between the microscopic view of particle behaviour and the macroscopic phenomenon of the set of particles makes this text one of the first to adopt the concepts of statistical mechanics to analyse production economics.

Farjoun and Machover (1983) base their view of a probabilistic political economy on an analogy with the kinetic theory of gases. From Maxwell–Boltzmann they take the idea that a system can reach a state of equilibrium without individual equilibria. The exchange of kinetic energy between particles is such that there is a re-equilibrium in the distribution of kinetic energy, which corresponds to an equilibrium in the velocity of the particles themselves. It can therefore be assumed that the system as a whole is stable despite micro-instability.

Karl Marx's and David Ricardo's labour theory of value is reinterpreted with the tools of mechanical statistics, namely, aggregates of agents, workers and capitalists. Farjoun and Machover (1983) focus on the formation of prices, expressed in relation to the hours of labour demanded. Prices are expressed as a Gaussian distribution characterised by a mean and a standard deviation from the mean.

Attention then shifts from prices to rates of profit, bearing in mind that, according to the kinetic analogy, there is no single rate of profit but a distribution of rates. From an economic point of view, it is interesting to analyse the spread of the profit rate, which Farjoun and Machover consider to be endogenous to the capitalist system. Technological innovations, organisational innovations, material markets and so on come to the fore. The result is a representation of a system that guarantees stable profits over time, given the complexity and randomness of micro-canonical relations.

Farjoun and Machover's work is important in this history not simply because it extended the analogy between economics and statistical mechanics but also because of the application to production. Although the term econophysics obviously does not appear in their text, the book is nevertheless an example of classical econophysics, where analytical tools borrowed from physics are used to analyse economic variables. Among these, labour, conventionally regarded as the source of value, occupies a prominent position because economics, while concerned with the study of social processes and structures, is actually concerned with how social labour is organised and performed and, ultimately, how the product of labour is distributed and put to different uses (1983: 85) (classical econophysics is provided with later insights in Cockshott et al., 2009).

This does not reduce the importance of other variables such as prices, according to the authors, linked to the labour content of the goods produced. The problem lies in the method used to derive prices, based on the existence of a uniform rate of profit, when it is probabilistic. The main thrust of the argument is to replace variables expressed by uniform values with probabilistic distributions, and this is not merely a methodological step.

The authors question the Marxian-inspired tendency of labour content to decline in the long run, bringing to the fore wages and prices, expressed here as random variables. What appears through the lens of probability and statistical mechanics is an interesting representation of the (capitalist) market. Prices are in equilibrium, but constantly changing as the quantities traded change. Similarly, the price of labour, the main cost of production, can change, but with a different distribution from that of product prices. The result is changing profits, which can also be interpreted in terms of a probability distribution. It should be noted, however, that this distribution is not a power or a Pareto law; rather, it is Gaussian.

Santa Fe Complexity

Econophysics is often associated not with a term that identifies a specific field of research, as is the case with income distribution or financial volatility, but with an approach to, or projection of, economic and financial phenomena: namely, 'complexity'. In this regard, the Santa Fe Institute is significant as the likely birthplace of complexity as a methodological approach. Operational since 1984, the Santa Fe Institute considers itself a research network on complex systems, whose results and research had a major influence on the birth of econophysics and continue to drive its development. Perhaps nowhere else have economists and physicists worked together on what can be called, abstractly, the 'complexity approach' (see Zurek 1989; Casdagli & Eubank, 1990; Weigend & Gershenfeld, 1994). It includes the Santa Fe artificial market and the minority game, models useful for understanding the behaviour of agents not guided by perfect rationality but acting inductively, adapting their behaviour to past experience.

The institute studies the behaviour of agents within a statistical mechanics framework, but shifts the focus from how agents act to why they do so. As we shall see, its analysis parallels and often overlaps with the focus on the macroscopic level. Indeed, although econophysics is primarily concerned with the macro level, the complexity of the relationship between macro and micro levels is crucial. Market behaviour is the result of choices made by agents, so assumptions such as 'zero intelligence', 'bounded rationality' and 'perfect rationality', considered in a complexity-based approach, are essential.

The approach to complexity adopted by the Santa Fe Institute is necessary to investigate questions that are difficult to deal with using the traditional mathematics of economics. In 1997, W. Brian Arthur, Steven Durlauf and David Lane created a list of six features that today are paradigmatic of complexity: dispersed interaction, that is, the interaction of many dispersed, possibly heterogeneous agents acting in parallel; no global controller, that is, no global entity controls the interactions; overarching hierarchical organisation, that is, the economy has many levels of organisation and interaction; continuous adaptation, that is, individual agents revise their behaviour according to their accumulated experience; perpetual novelty, because new markets, technologies, behaviours and institutions are constantly being created by niches; and out-of-equilibrium dynamics, because the economy operates far from optimal or global equilibrium due to continuous change (Arthur et al., 1997: 3–4; see also Arthur, 1994, 1999). These features did not immediately enter the lexicon of econophysics, but, one by one, they gradually emerged as the fundamental elements of a debate on the interaction of macro and micro levels, the subject of econophysics.

Kolkata Wealth Distribution

The story of the group in Kolkata, India, as told by Bikas Chakrabarti (2005; see also Chakrabarti & Sinha, 2021), is first and foremost the story of physicists' research into the distribution of income and wealth. The analogy between gas molecules and money was discussed in Kolkata in 1994, at a conference which brought together economists and physicists. In the conceptualisation of the monetary model from gas theory, the kinetic distribution of Gibbs gave way to a quantum distribution, based on Bose–Einstein. A second meeting was held in 1995 with a series of lectures known as 'Statphys–Kolkata', during one of which H. Eugene Stanley coined the term 'econophysics' to describe research on economic issues by physicists.

The kinetic model of the distribution of the particles of an (ideal) gas remains, with the added propensity to save characterising agents. According to

Chakrabarti (2005: 226), precisely the modelling of a random propensity to save captured the essential aspects of income distribution: the low level of income, the decline in average incomes, the power or Pareto law of high incomes. The interest in the Bose–Einstein quantum model arose precisely from the ability to bring together a large number of individuals with similar levels of savings in the same state. The Kolkata savings model requires memory of the past, fundamental because it precludes Markovian exchange, raising the level of sophistication of the exchange models based on kinetic analogy. The loss of savings in the course of exchange is able to plunge the agent into the tail of the distribution, where there is little or no wealth. The approach cultivated by the Kolkata group was consistent with the kinetic theory of gases, observing the random walks generated by the propensity to save, highlighting its stabilising effect (Chatterjee et al., 2004).

The Workshop on Economics with Heterogeneous Interacting Agents (WEHIA)

Physicists from India joined forces with economists from Italy in 1996, holding an informal meeting in Ancona, which led to the establishment of the WEHIA. Mauro Gallegati and Alan Kirman brought together economists, sociologists, biologists and physicists to explore a topic destined to become central to econophysics: the relationship between the formation and behaviour of economic aggregates and the interaction between the heterogeneous individuals that comprise them (Gallegati & Kirman, 2019).

The impetus for creating a permanent laboratory and publishing the *Journal of Economic Interaction and Coordination* came from the rejection of macroeconomic models that exclude heterogeneity and appear to be micro-founded on the sum of homogeneous individual behaviours. Conversely, heterogeneity being unquestionably important, research must focus on the aggregation of heterogeneous agents to account for aggregate dynamics arising from simple and complex individual actions and interactions (Auyang, 1998).

The WEHIA initiative is not based solely on the criticism of existing general equilibrium models. In particular, it is focused on the connection between individual interactions and visible, aggregate-level effects. The complexity of micro-relationships can determine macro-effects that exhibit a certain degree of regularity and simplicity (Aoki, 1996; Gallegati & Kirman, 1999). This idea of the aggregate as a result rather than the sum of interactions distinguishes econophysics from conventional macroeconomics.

By assuming that heterogeneity affects individual rationality and gives rise to phenomena such as networks, coordination and path dependence, econophysics is led to focus on the properties exhibited by systems, even in the absence of clear causal links to individual behaviour. The workshop did not end with the birth of econophysics but was repeated annually, fuelling research and debate on agent-based modelling and complex systems. Perhaps most importantly of all, the focus remained on the complex phenomenon of aggregation in economics.

Mantegna and Stanley's Introduction to Econophysics

Pareto's asymmetric distribution and Bachelier's random walk open the *Introduction to Econophysics*, the text by Rosario N. Mantegna and H. Eugene Stanley published in 2000, which symbolically marks the beginning of the new discipline. The short text outlines a broad research programme, with some previous research and other projects that later characterised the development of econophysics. Significantly, the baton of the new discipline was picked up by two physicists who focused on the area that most lent itself to the analogy with mechanical statistics, the stock market and finance in general. The main topics discussed are a perfect picture of the subject matter of early econophysics.

The starting point was the pricing of options (or other financial assets), a process to which the typical economic assumption of market efficiency applies, and the assertion that all immediately processed information contributes to price formation. However, since the nature of the information – 'noise' or 'information' – cannot be distinguished, any prediction for the return on financial assets seems to be ruled out, ridding the market efficiency hypothesis of its usefulness.

Setting aside the assumption of efficient markets in favour of a 'random walk', there is a problem with the probability density function (pdf) to which the random walk converges. While the Gaussian distribution is an important stable point of attraction, up to the point of assuming equality between the random walk and the Gaussian walk, other distributions are relevant, including the Lévy distribution, which can feature infinite variance and an asymptotic tail, and the power law, used to describe open systems.

In terms of the price time series to be analysed, a central aspect is stationarity, which, assuming that prices are independent stochastic variables, implies a uniformly distributed stochastic $x(t)$ process. This means that the pdf $P[x/t]$ is invariant over time. The authors' conclusion regarding stationarity is that time dependence phenomena, hence autocorrelation, are confined to the very short run. However, volatility, which is time-dependent, determines the asymptotic stationarity of financial markets.

The financial market requires further specification: not least the possible correlation and anti-correlation between pairs of stocks. Correlation can also be defined in terms of the metric distance (returns, prices) between two stocks. In the case of anti-correlation, the distance increases, especially in the long term. These aspects must be taken into account when modelling financial markets.

Given these premises, the question arises as to which statistical model should be used to represent the time evolution of prices in financial markets. Relevant clues come from the study of auto-correlation and the power spectrum, as well as from analyses of the asymptotic properties of price distributions. Gaussian models and truncated Lévi flights have both been proposed; however, there is no model that has been universally accepted to describe the stochastic process governing the time evolution of logarithmic prices (Mantegna & Stanley, 2000: 68). In continuous trading, price volatility and market turbulence play a crucial role and must be analysed from a scaling perspective, since different time horizons exhibit different statistical properties.

Mantegna and Stanley's analysis seems to suggest that the aspect that emerges most from the analogy between financial markets and physical scenarios is price volatility. The application of geometric Brownian motion (prices must always be positive) implies that volatility is constant, which is difficult to reconcile in finance and contradicts the requirement of full knowledge of the statistical properties of assets. Hence, Mantegna and Stanley recommended the deepest knowledge of the phenomena analysed (2000: 129).

If the market is the main subject of the disciplinary analogy between economics/finance and statistical mechanics – the application to production appearing premature or missed (see Gallegati et al., 2006) – it is necessary to understand its characteristics: stable, with predominantly random variables, subject to extreme events the timing of which is difficult to establish. To understand the market, it would also be necessary to determine whether the correlations between variables are solely short term or both short and long term.

Mantegna and Stanley's text provides an excellent picture of the consolidated, problematic and unresolved aspects today characterising the debate on the application of mechanical statistics to financial markets. They describe a research programme based on the macroscopic analysis of financial markets, accompanied by all the problematic aspects of the relationship between macroscopic stability and microscopic instability.

Part II A Quarter-Century of Econophysics (1999–2023)

4 Econophysics in a Scatter Plot

Mantegna and Stanley's (2000) text established the new discipline of econophysics. Since the end of the 1990s it has undergone a process of widespread dissemination through scientific journals – *Physica A*, *The European Physical*

Journal B, Statistical Mechanics, to name but three – and monographs. The second part of this Element illustrates the evolution of econophysics from the late 1990s to the present day, a period corresponding to roughly a quarter of a century.

To help the reconstruction, a scatter plot is set out in Figure 1, derived from the textual analysis of 1,080 articles on econophysics published between 1999 and 2023 in a wide range of scientific journals dedicated to physics and statistical mechanics. Textual analysis, based on the relative frequencies of words/n-grams, together with the use of correspondence analysis, makes it possible to derive a representation based essentially on the distance between words. Figure 1 shows the development of the lexicon over the period, here exemplified by a small number of words/n-grams. These appear close to the years in which they were most significant, offering an overview of the lexical evolution of econophysics in the more than a thousand articles analysed. The scatter plot can be read as a map (Greenacre, 2007) providing information about the development of the topics of econophysics. The figure is based not on a theoretical model or preconceived analysis but on the distribution of the vocabulary used in the articles over the period. Obviously, only the terms that are useful for the reconstruction are highlighted.

The scatter plot can be interpreted as follows. The central part (centroid) contains the words/n-grams that occur most frequently in the articles, which, significantly, are evenly distributed. 'Financial markets', for example, does not characterise the publications of a particular year but rather the whole period under consideration.

Figure 1 should be read from left to right, clockwise, in chronological sequence. The years are arranged to show the changes in content over time. The two percentages on the axes, which represent inertia in the language of correspondence analysis, can be interpreted as lexical variance. The higher the percentage, the greater the lexical and content change. For example, 10.00 per cent on the horizontal axis and 5.13 per cent on the vertical axis indicate a very modest lexical change.

However, the coordinates were chosen to express maximum linguistic variability and highlight the topics characterising each year during the period. Following the topics gives a good idea of the contents that have attracted the attention of econophysicists over the past quarter of a century, and hence forms a kind of short history of the discipline.

The topics highlighted in Figure 1 allow us to identify different phases in the lexical evolution of econophysics 1999–2007, 2008–2012, 2013–2017 and 2018–2023, respectively. This approach is useful mainly for narrative purposes and reflects only a loose concentration of topics. If issues driven by current

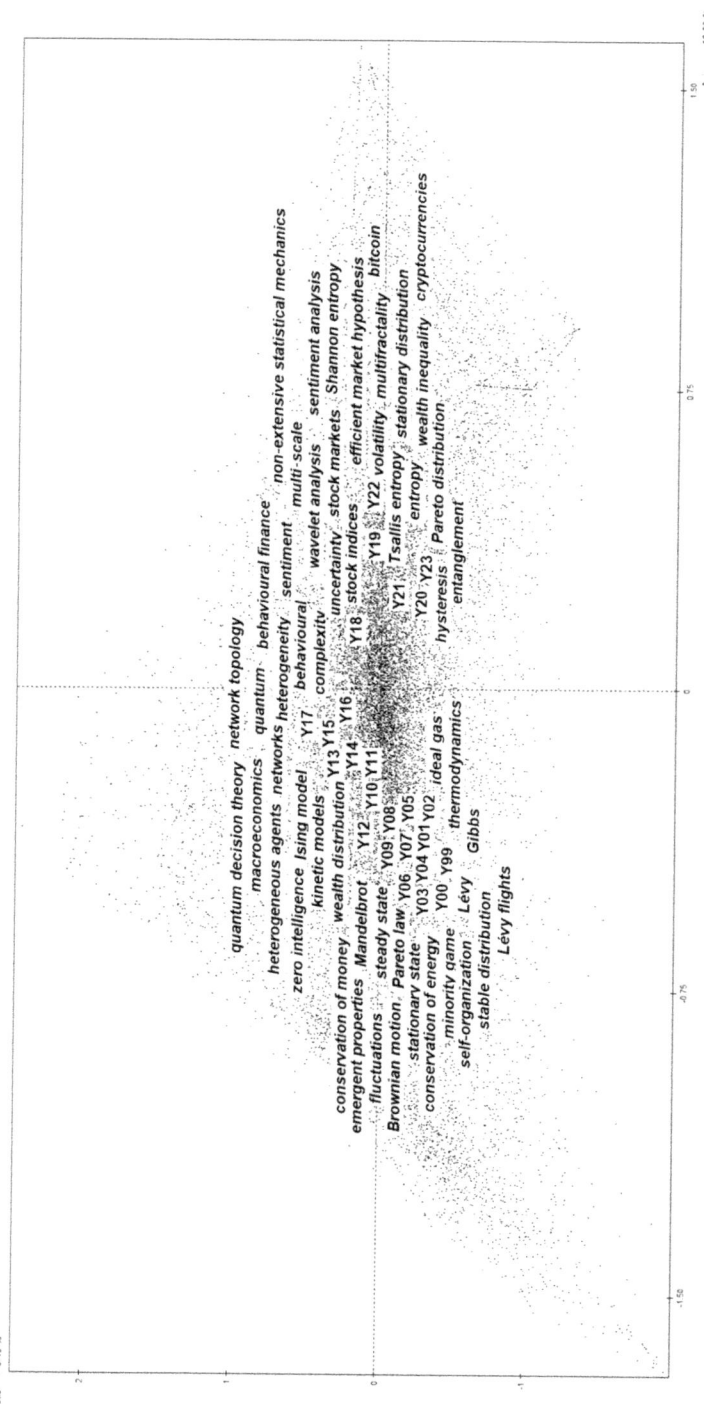

Figure 1 Econophysics in words (author's own elaboration).

events – such as financial crises or the emergence of cryptocurrencies – are set aside, econophysics exhibits a set of core issues that remains consistently central throughout the period.

5 1999–2007: Macroscopic and Microscopic Perspectives

Econophysics is based on statistical mechanics, as clearly stated by Mantegna and Stanley (2000), so one would expect the basic analyses of the new discipline to deal with the macroscopic level. This is certainly the case since econophysics continues to place the market at its centre and the market contains sets of variables, but it is true only to a certain extent given the massive attention paid to the economic agent. The macroscopic level remains central. The adoption of ideal gas models and postulates, such as stochastic independence, renders individual decisions and the interaction of agents virtually irrelevant. However, econophysics gradually reveals its unique nature: it looks at the macroscopic world while building a bridge to the microscopic.

For econophysics, the market is a space of more or less recurrent events that must be translated, as far as possible, into stylised facts which may concern individual agents grouped into aggregate variables. In particular, stylised facts must be supported by a large number of real or artificial observations, which limits econophysics to fields that can provide data. But it is precisely the vast amount of electronically recorded financial data that makes econophysics a laboratory for time series data and analytical methods (Marschinski & Kantz, 2002: 275–276).

In econophysics, the analogy with statistical mechanics involves a different relationship between macro and micro than in economics, not only because the mathematical and analytical tools are not the same but also because the explanatory role assigned by statistical mechanics to macro data disallows proceeding by additive processes. The priority given to the macroscopic level reveals a constant tension between the macro and the micro, stemming from the realisation that emergent properties, phenomena that manifest themselves at the macro level, are based on dynamics that may have a microscopic origin. Hence the focus on the macroscopic and the simultaneous investigation of the microscopic.

It is therefore understandable that macroscopic analysis, independent of the micro, depends on the ability to model stable macro conditions without perturbations, even when the markets analysed, especially financial markets, show diametrically opposed micro and macro trends. It is in the nature of statistical physics to infer changes in the macro states of matter through micro parameters (Yegorov, 2007: 144).

The relationship between macro and micro perspectives features throughout the first phase of the development of econophysics and guides subsequent developments (see Helbing, 2003). The reasons for this emphasis, beginning with the macro-level monetary perspective, are discussed in the following section.

Monetary Aggregates and the Conservation of Energy

Money is considered a non-perishable good that can be transformed and accumulated without loss to its nominal value; hence, it appears to be the economic good most suited to be treated by analogy with mechanical statistics. Victor M. Yakovenko and J. Barkley Rosser Jr note that in exchanges between individuals the amount of money changes hands but remains unchanged overall, and therefore the transfer of money can be considered analogous to the transfer of energy from one molecule to another in molecular collisions in a gas (Yakovenko & Rosser, 2009: 1706). Hence the reference to the conservation of money, which in a generalised form becomes the stationary distribution of money of the Boltzmann–Gibbs type (Yakovenko & Rosser, 2009: 1707 ff.). Money is the perfect example of a good to which the principle of the conservation of energy can be applied (see Dragulescu & Yakovenko, 2000).

Mircea Gligor and Margareta Ignat write that money can be seen as an extended variable like energy in physical systems, but its conservation appears as an idealisation similar to the 'isolated system' of physics (Gligor & Ignat, 2002: 126). The monetary theory of economists assumes a closed economy in the initial phase of the analysis. The problem of the impossibility of closed systems is similar to that of physics with solar energy, but the discussion revolves around the very meaning of the conservation of money.

Among scientists, the idea of the conservation of money as a parallel of the conservation of energy is controversial. Ning Ding et al. argue that if we consider an exchange between any two agents in a closed economy where money is conserved in the same way as an elastic collision between two bodies in an ideal gas, it can be shown that, no matter how evenly money is initially distributed between agents, subsequent exchanges will eventually lead to a stable distribution of money (Ding et al., 2003: 149). Adrian A. Dragulescu and Yakovenko say that they are interested in the stationary distribution, which corresponds to the state of thermodynamic equilibrium. In this state, an individual agent's money fluctuates enormously, but the overall probability distribution does not change (Dragulescu & Yakovenko, 2000: 724). They add that the stationary distribution condition is of interest because it enables the study of non-equilibrium phenomena (Dragulescu & Yakovenko, 2000: 729), whereas thermodynamic equilibrium in the economy is difficult to identify.

On the other hand, as Joseph L. McCauley says, there is no reliable analogue of energy in economics, and there are good reasons why it seems difficult to construct a meaningful thermodynamic analogy (McCauley, 2007). Thermodynamic equilibrium does not have a direct application in socio-economic sciences, since it seems to be absent from markets and economic production. Non-equilibrium and irreversible thermodynamics attract more attention (Tsirlin et al., 2003). Bertrand M. Roehner highlights the differences between physics and the social sciences. In physics, even empirical consistency between models and basic principles, such as the conservation of energy, is a guarantee that the model really describes what is happening. By contrast, in sociology and economics there are no rules or principles equivalent to those in physics that can be tested with a high degree of accuracy. This fundamental asymmetry leads to a profound difference in modelling practices between physics and the social sciences (Roehner, 2008: 263).

The principle of the conservation of energy or money is not a sufficient condition for macroscopic equilibrium. However, by shaping the construction of models, it influences not only how micro- and macro-level variables are related but also the transfer of concepts and tools from statistical mechanics into economics and finance. In this context, monetary aggregates are particularly well suited to the assumption of an invariant overall money stock, which is redistributed among individuals through their interactions – interactions that are governed not necessarily by rationality but by a range of factors, including chance.

Fluctuations and Extreme Events

Micro- and macro-dynamics are fundamental to the interpretation of phase transitions in markets, especially financial markets, often described by analogy with those of physical materials. The Ising model tells us that a magnetic dipole moment or 'spin' interacts (exchanges energy) with its neighbours. The system can thus move from a state of spin alignment to one of alienation, which is a phase transition (Jain & Buckley, 2006). Neighbourhood, as a crucial element for magnetic exchange, is a concept that is also widely used in the analysis of financial markets because of its information content (Cajueiro & Soares De Camargo, 2006). Hence, an agent is defined, among other things, by the node or position it occupies in the market and the relationships it has with other nodes.

It follows that the analysis of markets as collective phenomena in economics and social sciences is a challenge for statistical physicists, not unlike problems such as understanding how spontaneous magnetisation can arise in a magnetic system. In both cases, it is important to understand how the effects of interactions occurring at the microscopic level can accumulate at the macroscopic level (De Martino & Marsili, 2006). The frequent reference to the spin-glass model, a generalisation of Ising's model, shows that if, on the one hand, the aim is to analyse the temporal evolution of macroscopic order parameters (correlation and response functions) without referring to the microscopic process of the individual agent, on the other hand, the decision-making element cannot be ignored (Heimel & De Martino, 2001). The goal is to understand disorder in condensed matter as well as in individual financial exchanges, where agents do not follow a paradigm of rational expectations but act inductively, adapting their behaviour to past experience (Giardina & Bouchaud, 2003) and taking into account the behaviour of their neighbours.

Financial fluctuations that drive phase transitions can be the result of these individual behaviours. As Didier Sornette (2002) points out, financial fluctuations are not limited to normal fluctuations around the fundamental price but concern the behaviour of the market on days of extreme gains or losses (Lillo & Mantegna, 2000). Vasiliki Plerou et al.'s (2000: 443) argument that stock price fluctuations occur in all dimensions is powerful. Similar to earthquakes, small fluctuations can lead to drastic events such as market crashes. Plerou et al. conclude that the distribution of price fluctuations decays with a power-law tail that is well outside the stable Lévy regime, and describe fluctuations that differ by up to eight orders of magnitude.

Fluctuations characterised by peaks immediately raise at least two sets of problems – their representation and their treatment – since the analyst's aim is to be able to predict the future evolution of the prices of financial assets and thus of investment returns. The representation of fluctuations recalls the importance attached to Mandelbrot in terms of the inclusion of so-called extreme phenomena. Mandelbrot spoke of price peaks, which gave substance to his theory of heavy tails with non-finite variance. This phenomenology of 'peaks' focuses on the intensity and time interval between price changes to determine their magnitude. The acceptance or rejection of peaks determines the theoretical construction of data interpretation. As we have seen, according to Pareto, asymptotic curves – power law – are assumed to represent the distribution of data, and the assumption of extreme events implies strong asymptotic tails. However, the frequency of these events is such that they cannot be included among random phenomena and their inclusion becomes a matter of a priori choice rather than observation.

Crucially, the possibility of extreme economic shocks of the same magnitude as natural phenomena such as earthquakes is mimicked, as said earlier, by the assumption of a non-finite variance, as suggested by Lévy's flights. In contrast, the choice of a truncated Lévy procedure, that is, the imposition of an exponential tail 'decay', excludes extreme phenomena from the analysis (see Ivanov et al., 2001). The adoption of exponential decay reflects a preference for short 'Brownian' motions over long phases of Lévy flights (Wang & Hui, 2001).

Stanley et al. (2002) question the inclusion of extreme shocks in the analysis, although they are aware that the adoption of the truncated Lévy process implies independent and identically distributed stochastic variables, a characteristic not always found in nature. On the one hand, there is stochastic independence and an approximation to a Gaussian distribution; on the other hand, there are independent stochastic variables which preclude scale invariance, that is, the possibility of retaining the same properties regardless of the level of aggregation. Stanley et al. address this by looking for 'scalar' models that allow for different levels of price volatility. This could be done by using a 'power law' that allows for the externalisation of standard deviations, or by observing the relationship between economic organisation and fluctuations. It should be noted that these are empirical observations which, at the time Stanley wrote (Stanley et al., 2002: 2129), lacked a theoretical basis for exploration.

The counterpoint between Brownian motion, as a geometric variation distributed around a mean, and Lévy's flights, which involve sudden and unpredictable events as well as non-finite means and variance, cannot fail to inform the study of stock markets. The analytical result often obtained is the coexistence of different distributions within the same space (see Górski et al., 2002), or according to prices and yields, often with multifractality, that is, different exponents according to scale.

The key is the treatment of fluctuations, a crucial issue in econophysics. Obviously, the stochastic independence mentioned earlier simplifies the computation and interpretation of the four statistical 'moments'. Given this independence, the random walk, a continuous-time generalisation of Brownian motion, can be reduced to a Gaussian representation, which is much more manageable than Lévy flights in terms of predicting variables. The problem is the correspondence with reality.

Independence versus correlation is almost a mantra in financial observation. The issue of correlation came to the fore as the literature on stock returns grew. In the first phase, the focus on short-term returns seemed to be gaining ground, fuelled by the random walk hypothesis, which asserts the randomness of stock market returns. However, the alternative hypothesis, the dependence of today's returns on the returns of previous periods, was also rapidly gaining ground, and with it the need to complement research on short-term with research on long-term dependence. Dependence over long time horizons can be interpreted as correlation, or even auto-correlation, if, for example, it is assumed that a change of one type is normally followed by a change of the opposite sign in the same asset (see Grau-Carles, 2000).

In its early days, econophysics focused more on short-term correlations. By measuring the magnitude of price changes in absolute value or the square of price changes, the associated short-term (even several months) correlations can be described by a power law. This is noted by Stanley et al. (2001: 127), who add that what is important is not only the price variance but also the number of financial transactions in a given period. This last point is interesting because it implies that correlation phenomena depend in part on the decision to make or not to make investment transactions.

Finally, looking at the problems that arise from analysing money and financial markets together, the constraint that provides an exclusively macro perspective on markets is their isolation: isolation from energy/currency flows, from unpredictable and extreme events, from memories of the past and conditioning from other markets or market scales. These constraints keep the system in a stable state. As we shall see, econophysics has developed in relation to the maintenance or relaxation of these constraints.

Macroscopic Steady State

The aim is to identify the conditions for macroscopic stability, understood as a situation in which macroscopic properties respond to micro-level perturbations while the overall distribution remains unchanged. Under certain conditions, the Pareto distribution can represent the system's long-term stable state. At the same time, the Pareto distribution raises the issue of stationarity, that is, the constancy of mean and variance. There may be an evolution where the distribution changes but remains unchanged on average, identifying a steady state condition. If it remains unchanged according to Markov chains, the distribution appears to be aperiodic and irreducible (ergodic). It is important to understand how the properties of a system remain constant over time despite transitions at the micro level, in particular whether they depend on previous states. It is clear that assuming 'ideal gas' conditions, with particles moving at constant speed and not exchanging energy, the steady state extends from the micro to the macro level.

This explains the use of ideal gas and a stationary model by Kolkata researchers involved in income distribution analysis. But the key word in the transition from microscopic perturbations to macroscopic steady state is self-organisation. It is no coincidence that the Kolkata tradition, citing Arnab Chatterjee et al. (2003) among others, uses a model in which agents with a propensity to save are modelled on ideal gas particles. The propensity to save is the key feature for self-organisation. A uniform propensity to save leads to an exponential distribution, while different propensities to save lead to a Pareto distribution (Chatterjee et al., 2003). In this view, steady state is a matter of self-organisation, that is, it is assumed that the sum of the random walks of individuals, given stochastic independence, leads to a steady state distribution.

In 2002, Chun-Bin Yang and Xu Cai wrote that a system self-adjusts from any initial state to a steady state through complex non-linear interactions between components. The steady state can be represented by a power-law distribution, which can be seen as a fingerprint of a system in a critical self-organised state. What remains to be done is to investigate the internal correlations (Yang & Cai, 2002: 774). The steady state is therefore a product of the interaction and evolution of agents. For example, in a growing economy, the size of firms may change according to a power law (Delli Gatti et al., 2004; Fujiwara et al., 2004). Interestingly, the system can evolve into a critical state while still satisfying the conditions of a steady state. The minority game itself shows that the population can 'win globally' and consistently reach a stable configuration in which all agents obtain a positive pay-off (Fagiolo & Valente, 2005). Hence, in order to understand macroscopic stability, it may be necessary to analyse the micro perspective, or rather the self-organising capacity of agents at the micro level (Aoki & Yoshikawa, 2007).

Minority Game

Self-organisation is a fundamental part of the *minority game*. Stanley et al. (2001) note that investment decisions help determine financial returns. The dilemma of whether or not to buy a security, knowing that an increase in the number of buyers will reduce its profitability, becomes, in the early complexity literature, the 'minority game', that is, a game involving the choice between two options, which, in Arthur's original example of the El Farol restaurant, is the choice between attending or not attending a musical event in a limited space. In the case of the patrons of the musical event in the restaurant, as in the case of the purchase of financial assets, it would be convenient for the purchase to remain the preserve of a limited group of players.

In the 'minority game', agents have to choose from a pool of strategies made available to them in order to achieve a certain goal in a financial or other market (see Galla et al., 2003). At first sight, the economic agent appears, in relation to the market as a system, as a price taker whose investment strategies depend on the circulation of information. However, alternative formulations can be developed in which the pay-off function is extended beyond standard minority games, allowing agents to switch opportunistically between minority and majority positions (see Andersen & Sornette, 2003). A more sophisticated version of the minority game is the grand canonical minority game (Ferreira et al., 2005), populated by heterogeneous producers (agents trading in the market) and equally heterogenous speculators (trying to profit from the market).

In addition to the typology of agents, the grand canonical minority game introduces a further option to the two – buy or sell – inherent in the classical game: opt out of the game, that is, do not take the risk. The idea is to give agents a benchmark so that they remain in the market only if they perform well (Challet et al., 2001). The decision is complicated by the fact that for speculators, entry then exit would lead to losses. Peaks and troughs in the market are thus caused by the concentrated actions of speculators. The grand canonical minority game shows that, without speculators, product prices follow a random walk, while stylised facts disappear when a sufficient number of speculators impacts on the market (Challet et al., 2001).

However, the most interesting phenomenon of the minority game model is the emergence of a self-organisational phase that manifests itself as coordination when the standard deviation of participation, the volatility, becomes smaller than in the random choice game (Galstyan & Lerman, 2002). Emergent coordination is a question of memory and strategic space, and above all of using local rather than global information.

The message is that the macroscopic perspective cannot ignore the microscopic where agents spontaneously organise themselves. This aspect gradually crept in after the initial consolidation phase of econophysics, and is fully compatible with the macroscopic dimension of econophysics. Self-organisation and emergent coordination are expressions of microscopic dynamism, which is then translated into macroscopic stability. Crucially, there is no macroscopic regulator to guide the micro-behaviour. What modifies the original approach, especially the pivot on stochastic independence, is the presence of interactions from coordination and self-organisation, and these require modelling with a great degree of freedom.

Agent-based models, often used since the early 2000s, simulate a market of interacting agents, whether firms (Ikeda et al., 2007) or traders (Alfi et al., 2009), these being autonomous and potentially heterogeneous agents. The interaction, simple or complex, determines the properties of the system at the macro level, and these are referred to as emergent properties. Different properties can be obtained during the simulation by modifying the interaction rules. The focus is on agents and the outcome of decision-making processes, on stylised facts produced by interactive mechanisms, leaving room for random choices that ignore the information available or disregard consequences (Brandouy et al., 2012).

6 2008–2012: Distribution Centrality

Income Distribution

Individual events may be unique, and micro-level instabilities can affect macro-level stability; nevertheless, macroscopic behaviour must be represented independently of specific events, at an aggregate level. Against this background, between 2008 and 2012, econophysics moved towards increasing complexity, consolidating its anchoring in statistical mechanics, reinforcing its macroscopic orientation and focusing on dynamics emerging from the analysis of large datasets in the search for stylised facts and emergent patterns. It remains to be seen to what extent the interaction of many agents can be understood without studying individual agents.

Distribution is a key word, present from the outset of econophysics, albeit accentuated in the 2008–2012 period. The term 'income distribution' is not highlighted in Figure 1 because of its position in the middle, surrounded by the terms cutting across the entire period. Hence, income and wealth distribution comprise a 'sub-field' of econophysics where the study of aggregates remains pivotal and is related to, if not overlapping with, sociophysics (Chakrabarti et al., 2006).

The macroscopic view can be organised in two ways (see Banerjee & Yakovenko, 2010). The first focuses on macroscopic variables, such as the money stock, without examining the microeconomic assumptions. The principle of the conservation of energy and money remains central to this view. The second view shows econophysics as a discipline that investigates macroscopic variables, primarily markets, without neglecting the microscopic. Both are present in analysis of the distribution of income and wealth.

The first perspective, confined to macroeconomic variables, holds that under a conservation principle applied to money, the asymmetric power-law distribution arises not from specific socio-economic factors but from probabilistic 'collisions' among agents. The distribution can be highly unequal, even if the agents are statistically equal (Yakovenko, 2016: 3314). Statistical equilibrium is given by an exponential function. This is crucial because, in this way, skewed distributions – first and foremost the power law due to its invariant properties – become central to econophysics. The Maxwell–Boltzmann kinetic model is fully imported into economics and finance.

According to the second view, the income models are based on different behavioural assumptions: the transfer of a portion of income, savings, debt, taxation. Although the start condition is often an equal distribution of income/wealth, the end condition is characterised by skewed distributions with more or less pronounced tails.

Despite the attraction of a statistical-mechanical representation of the exchange equation, the focus on exchanges between individuals increased with time. Following John Angle (2006), Victor Yakovenko and Barkley Rosser (2009) studied individual decisions to transfer a variable part of income, partly due to price fluctuations, and, alongside transfers and savings, introduce borrowing, interpreted as negative money, allowed by central banks (a large money supply). The result of the simulation is a gamma or exponential distribution and a heavy tail at the bottom. A comparison with the actual data on income distribution shows the remarkable stability of the lower part of the curve, which does not change despite the gradual increase in average income in nominal dollars. This finding suggests that the distribution at the bottom is in 'thermal' statistical equilibrium (Yakovenko & Rosser, 2009: 1716). In contrast, the addition of the economic growth variable shifts the focus to the upper tail of the power law.

Continuing a long tradition of research, the Kolkata group drew attention to savings decisions, the introduction of which into kinetic exchange models makes it possible to highlight how self-organisation is an important emerging feature (Chatterjee, 2009: 597). The assumption that agents only receive money from other agents by exchange leads to the claim that the principle of saving can be confirmed both bilaterally and systemically. But self-organisation has a clear meaning in terms of income distribution. Agents begin to interact with each other, leading the system towards a stable form close to a skewed distribution, which can be a gamma, Pareto or power-law distribution.

It is also true that the resulting negatively sloped curves are open to interpretation. In income distributions that include savings, the central portion of the wealth distribution may follow a Gibbs distribution, while the extremes – the tails – exhibit, on the one hand, dispersion and, on the other, concentration. In this case, a Pareto distribution provides an appropriate fit for the tails rather than for the distribution as a whole. One interpretation of the tails, scarcity and concentration is based on the absence or accumulation of savings, where saving is an expression of self-interest (see Chatterjee & Chakrabarti, 2007). Attributing 'savings propensities' to agents (Chatterjee & Sen, 2010) or changing their savings parameters (Patriarca et al., 2010) determines the intensity of their exchanges and, consequently, the distribution itself. Socio-economic interaction takes place in the market, which itself becomes the place where skewed distributions are formed.

Finally, precisely because they are able to shed light on the different laws underlying the distribution of income between the richest and the poorest (two distributions: Clementi et al., 2007), the more descriptive models remain fundamental to the analysis of income and wealth distribution proposed by econophysicists (Clementi et al., 2008; Clementi & Gallegati, 2016). In this way, the inequality typical of any asymmetric distribution, with its ethical connotations, is highlighted as an additional element of complexity in the processes of self-organisation.

Power Law

In 2001, Jean-Philippe Bouchaud pointed out that physicists are often fascinated by power laws. This is because these laws are able to describe complex and collective phenomena in a universal way, largely independent of the microscopic details of the phenomena themselves. Thus, the laws of power emerge from collective action and transcend individual specificities (Bouchaud, 2001: 105). It should be added that the data show a power-law trend immediately adjacent to the critical phase transition points. An observation often made by econophysicists is that the distributions converge to the power law regardless of the specificity of individual behaviour. Paul M. Anglin (2005: 229–230) writes that wealth distribution models developed by econophysicists are interesting because they use a process not previously considered to explain a macro phenomenon. As it becomes clear that almost all systems composed of large numbers of interacting units are likely to exhibit power-law behaviour (Stanley et al., 2007: 288), the power law becomes a focal point from which to analyse critical stages and adopt scaling as a conceptual framework. Just as Pareto questioned the cause of the asymmetric distribution of income, economic physicists attribute the ability to generate a power law to exchange.

Citing Mark Newman (2005), Franck Jovanovic and Christophe Schinckus note that any work in econophysics seeks to demonstrate through empirical evidence that the phenomenon under study is governed by a power law (2017: 63). They insist on the exportability of the power law to other fields, such as finance (Jovanovic & Schinckus, 2017: 63–65). Unlike the Gaussian, the power law can be taken as a natural starting point for renormalisation or generalisation since it retains its form under additive, multiplicative and polynomial transformations (Jovanovic & Schinckus, 2017: 96–97). In its ubiquity, the power law brings together the two main areas of analysis in economics: the distribution of income and wealth, and the study of markets, including fluctuations and long memory phenomena. The convergence towards the law of power as a law of distribution for social phenomena, which are by definition aggregates, becomes paradigmatic to the point where observations at the microscopic level are no longer considered necessary to support exponents of scale and universal laws. Interactions, multiplicative effects, preferential attachment and self-organisation – phenomena typical of complex systems – are often not explicitly modelled, yet they underlie the emergence of power-law distributions, which therefore reflect a cause or, rather, a complex and inextricable set of causes.

However, despite convergence, the power law is not without its problems. Bouchaud himself notes that power-law models can contain multiplicative noise and have non-universal exponents depending on the choice of parameter values (2001: 21). The law of power is probably not the universal law that some have claimed it to be, but it is nevertheless a very powerful concept because of its potential applications to a wide variety of natural and man-made systems (Slanina, 2014: 346).

Like the Boltzmann distribution, the power law is used as a synonym for market efficiency in other than kinetic models, such as Lotka–Volterra dynamic foundation models (Malcai et al., 2002), often used by physicists. While relating the incomes/wealth of the poorest sectors to those of the richest sectors of society as a function of a single parameter, for example the ratio of the constant component – social security – to the variable component – investment – these models exclude the assumption of abnormal returns and assume that the market guarantees a 'fair price', giving rise to a stable power-law distribution. It is therefore possible to achieve a state analogous to thermal equilibrium (stationarity and stability), provided the above market conditions apply.

Power laws imply the autonomy of the macroscopic level, which can be an object of analysis hypothesising *zero-intelligence agents*, that is, agents that are not strategic and do not follow optimisation rules. A significant application of the zero-intelligence hypothesis is the study of orders in liquid securities following large intra-day price changes in financial markets. Bence Toth et al. (2009) analyse the relaxation effects of order curves after a spike. This is a slow phenomenon that can be described by a power law with a low exponent. In order to understand whether or not this phenomenon is the result of strategic behaviour by agents, the authors adopt a zero-intelligence order flow model and conclude that slow relaxations may not be the result of strategic agent behaviour but, rather, due to other factors such as market or institutional mechanisms (Toth et al., 2009: 506). The function of zero-intelligence agents is to study the extent to which the decisions of individual agents influence the evolution of the phenomena under study and the creation of power-law distributions. In other words, to determine how much micro-dynamics influence macro-dynamics.

By assigning risk and savings preferences on a mean-variance basis, kinetic approaches are able to generate realistic Pareto tails in the stationary distribution of wealth (Düring et al., 2008). Clearly, the size of the tail is not irrelevant, especially for predicting rare phenomena, and requires the careful definition of the factors influencing the rate of re-savings and determining taxation in prediction models.

7 2013–2017: Harnessing Uncertainty

An Increasingly Complex Market

At the beginning of the third phase in Figure 1 running from 2013 to 2017, econophysics consolidated research on market fluctuations in the direction of power laws or the like. The process of consolidating the power law as an economic 'distribution' thus intensified, even when applied to non-Pareto domains (exponent different from 1.5) (Gabaix, 2009, 2016). However, the use of power laws has become more sophisticated. Thomas Lux and Simone Alfarano point out that after one of the most widespread discoveries in financial economics in the last decade, that large price changes follow a power law, the attention of the scientific community has shifted to a second power law regarding the time-dependent structure of volatility (Lux & Alfarano, 2016: 3). The use of the power law to highlight the temporal structure of volatility opens up a broad reflection on correlation and auto-correlation phenomena in financial markets (Richmond et al., 2014). The power law makes it possible to highlight decay processes, the slowness or rapidity of which is an indication of the greater or lesser memory of the past (Kristoufek, 2013, 2014; Miccichè, 2013). Another important aspect highlighted by the volatility time series, already present but of increasing relevance, is the multifractal nature of cross-correlations, opening up measures of market efficiency (Xie et al., 2015) and risk (Gallegati, 2016).

Beyond the analogy with statistical mechanics, a number of insights bring econophysics close to other approaches in economics and finance. The frequent distinction between the upper and lower parts of the income distribution, each responding to different distributions (da Silva Junior & de Figueirêdo, 2014; Shaikh et al., 2014), featured significantly in the period. The same starting position of agents – more or less wealthy – through behaviour aimed at consolidating the status quo may explain the persistence of social inequity (Moukarzel, 2013). However, there was a gradual trend towards micro-founding the distribution by analysing financial flows between agents and their propensity to save or give away part of their income (Zanin et al., 2016).

One element of change that emerges strongly in this third phase is a focus on heterogeneity, particularly in terms of the agents that make up the social and economic system (Zhou et al., 2017). This is not only true for income savers; the set of investors is in many ways also a highly heterogeneous system. This heterogeneity leads us to boundedly rational agents (Franke & Asada, 2008) and to the hierarchical structure of individual investors' trading profiles (Musciotto et al., 2016).

From particles to living agents, one might say. A shift that only seemingly contradicts another important conceptual development in econophysics during this period: the adoption of quantum mechanics as a parallel paradigm to statistical mechanics. As we shall see, the individual element is central to quantum economics and quantum finance.

Quantum Mechanics

The emergence of quantum mechanics is shown by the numerous associations with 'quantum' ventured: not only 'quantum physics' and 'quantum mechanics' but also 'quantum decision theory', 'quantum game', 'quantum finance', 'quantum walk', 'quantum strategy' and so on. Quantum mechanics partly changed the perspective with which econophysics views particles and, by analogy, agents (Orrell, 2020). The reason for the change in perspective was the need to express, formally or otherwise, the familiar uncertainty of markets, especially financial markets. The relationships between the properties of the system remain probabilistic, the difference being that the probability is an intrinsic property of the quantum system being analysed and is represented by the square of the modulus of the wave function. This wave function replaces the point observation of the particle, since the properties of the particle can now only be expressed probabilistically. The price of an option can be seen not to follow a random path or Brownian motion, as in the analogy with statistical mechanics, but to follow different probabilistically expressed trajectories (states). The financial market encompasses all possible trajectories associated with the price of an asset.

The same particles whose collisions were theorised by analogy are now replaced by discrete units of energy, or quanta. Energy itself loses its material character, so to speak, and becomes a factor determining processes (Mirowski, 1989: 87) or the degree of collective trading activity by investors (Ahn et al., 2017: 6). The new imperative is to focus on quantities of energy, on electric charges and spins, and to treat asset prices as processes. And more than between quanta of energy and agents, the significant analogy is between quanta and prices, returns, investments, incomes, capital and economic variables. The market populated by quantum entities thus becomes a market of uncertain economic variables whose values can only be expressed probabilistically. There remains the difference between the discrete dimension of quanta and the mostly continuous dimension of financial and economic quantities, which needs to be made explicit.

Accordingly, quantum mathematics follows. The use of operators and Hilbert space marks a break with the mathematics of statistical mechanics. Undoubtedly, quantum mechanics shifts the focus from ensembles of individuals making choices to discrete but abstract entities influencing each other.

The contribution to the study of financial markets by the quantum approach was very significant in the period under examination. On the one hand, quantum agents have simultaneous, multiple and potentially conflicting preferences and experience conflicting emotions (models that attempt to capture the complexity and nuance of human behaviour). On the other hand, a single action should be treated as a quantum harmonic oscillator, excited by external information and damped towards its fundamental state, but also characterised by a small scale of persistent fluctuations (Meng et al., 2015). As a result, there is a strictly probabilistic dimension to the agents themselves, defined on a quantum basis.

To explore the characteristics of the analogy with quantum mechanics, the notion of *entanglement* is fundamental. Quantum entanglement means that measuring one state also measures a second state, albeit at a distance. The idea that the state of one agent can similarly determine the state of a second agent is interesting for its potential applications in finance and other fields (Zabaleta et al., 2017; Ardenghi, 2021). If kinetic theory is based on collisions between particles, quantum theory replaces them with entanglement, the mutual influence of quantum agents.

According to Didier Sornette (2014: 9), since around 2006 a strand of literature has developed that borrows the concept of interference and entanglement from quantum mechanics to try to explain the fallacies and paradoxes plaguing standard decision theories. Consistently, Vyacheslav I. Yukalov and Didier Sornette (2015, 2016a, 2016b) developed a quantum-based decision theory, claiming not that the brain operates on the basis of quantum physics but that each individual decision is inherently probabilistic and aims to unravel a network of propositions. Yukalov and Sornette's argument seeks to demonstrate the active rather than the passive nature of economic agents (2017), a far cry from early econophysics, which focused on ensembles of indistinct particles.

This seems particularly true for the in-depth study of quantum strategies and quantum games, in which players can choose several strategies simultaneously (Iqbal et al., 2015; Pawela, 2016). In general, the use of tools from quantum mechanics deepens the analysis of market uncertainty embedded in the properties of the wave function. Short-term stock market returns are brought back into long-term equilibrium. Market focus is provided by attention to the agents and their ability to interpret contextual or market uncertainty. Moreover, quantum tools increase the circulation of information and communication in markets, especially stock markets (see Bagarello & Haven, 2015; Ardenghi, 2023).

Kwangwon Ahn et al. (2017) argue that quantum models have an advantage over traditional models of stock returns in that they incorporate market conditions into stock returns, an aspect captured by the potential term in the Hamiltonian – that is, in the function representing the total energy of the system.

If stocks are considered as oscillators, changes in prices and returns cannot be explained by the classical theory of stock price fluctuations, but must be interpreted in light of the uncertainty of irrational transactions. In fact, assuming perfectly rational transactions, it is possible to determine the share price with certainty and thus to take into account the real value of the share. The oscillator hypothesis, on the other hand, implies an irrationality of transactions that is the source of further price fluctuations and thus of a small but persistent finite uncertainty (Meng et al., 2015). The result is a probabilistic description that is useful for exploring the 'random evolution' of stock prices (Ahn et al., 2017: 3), even if it is a randomness that is mathematically embedded in the equations expressing quantum fluctuations.

Evidently, quantum entanglement shifts attention away from aggregates to individual entities (quanta) and the relationships between them. It begs the question of whether quantum finance is a complementary discipline to econophysics rather than part of it. Although the similarity between mechanical statistics and quantum mechanics is undeniable, they appear to give rise to different approaches in the economic/financial sphere: the former, macroscopic, focusing on the behaviour of large sets of particles/agents; the latter concerned with the uncertainty characterising the microscopic, especially financial variables, in light of mutual influence.

Network Analysis

Quantum entanglement refocused attention on the connections between entities, whether microscopic or macroscopic, an aspect that had perhaps been somewhat neglected by econophysics. This interest was confirmed at the time by another discipline entering the field of econophysics: network analysis. According to Frantisek Slanina, the numerous interdependencies we find in society can be expressed as a set of networks that map certain aspects of pairwise interactions between human persons or collective entities, or even products of human activities (2014: 222). Leonardo Bargigli and Gabriele Tedeschi add that since network theory is concerned with the structure of interaction within systems with a multiplicity of agents, it is naturally interested in the statistical equilibrium of these same systems, which, brought back into a framework, brings the macroeconomics it represents closer to the theoretical approach of statistical physics and stochastic combinatorial processes (2014: 2). And from a quantum point of view, the continuous exchange of information necessary for the formation of decision-makers' judgements forms a kind of information network based on quantum rules, in which collective decisions evolve over time as a result of information exchange (Yukalov et al., 2018).

'Network' is a fundamental concept that enables understanding the complex interrelationships and dependencies in an economic system (Aoyama et al., 2017). To assess the weight of this concept in econophysics, it may be useful to recall its multiple terminological uses: 'complex networks', 'neural networks', 'social networks', 'network topology', 'random networks' and so on. Beyond the collision of gaseous particles of kinetic theory, the focus of network analysis is on the structural relationships among entities, agents and others. It is embedded in the analogy between statistical physics and finance/economics. Financial markets comprise complex networks with assets, countries and banks as nodes; measuring these relationships is crucial for an understanding of the functioning and critical aspects of financial markets.

Network analysis includes the minimal spanning tree, introduced by Mantegna (1999), to classify stock market shares, including in different countries, providing information on stock markets and financial networks, or on minimal subsets of assets maximising diversification while minimising risk. The distance between time series is used to construct taxonomies reducing price and return fluctuations by directing trades. Papers on this topic were more numerous after the 2008 financial crisis (Gilmore et al., 2008; Di Matteo et al., 2010; Bocci et al., 2014; Djauhari & Gan 2015, 2016), as volatility increased in the stock markets of several countries.

'Complex networks' appears more frequently than 'complex system', encompassing not only the financial world but also production and trade networks. It is no coincidence that 'macroeconomics' is another of the terms characterising the 2013–2017 period. It is easy to argue that econophysics opens up to macroeconomics precisely because of the complex interactions presupposed by networks. The reference to communities of productive networks shifts econophysics towards a spatial dimension, which inevitably draws attention to the multiple links connecting production or financial nodes internationally. These nodes include institutions, firms, industries, central banks and agents. Econophysics is thus enriched by macro-econophysics, an important sub-field that opens up opportunities and raises challenges. In 2016, Paul Ormerod noted that there was a great opportunity for econophysicists in the field of macroeconomics, as traditional (dynamic stochastic general equilibrium (DSGE)) models were seen as unsatisfactory by both policymakers and mainstream economists (2016: 3288).

Has this opportunity been seized? In the same year, McCauley noted that although the vast majority of econophysics publications were devoted to financial issues, some focused on macroeconomics, industrial economics and international economics (McCauley et al., 2016). Indeed, econophysics has remained predominantly a discipline devoted to finance, with dips into the real economy. Certainly, the area of the real economy that has most attracted physicists is macroeconomics. This is due to the fact that, at the macro level, 'stylised facts' (long-run growth of GDP per capita, excess volatility of investment) can be found, compatible with the econophysics approach (Berg et al., 2015; Lux & Alfarano, 2016).

Network analysis applied to regional and international economics was favoured by the theoretical context of the mid 2010s, leading to more research on macroeconomics and the real economy, although this was only a temporary phenomenon (Fagiolo, 2010; Garas et al., 2012; Kocakaplan et al., 2012). As early as 2007, Mircea Gligor and Marcel Ausloos provided a detailed explanation of reduced interest in macroeconomics. In addition to the frequent reference to the difficulty of experimentation in economics, the focus is on the number of explanatory variables, which is significantly higher in macroeconomics than in the natural sciences. Macroeconomic time series are short and noisy, often covering long periods, which raises the problem of stationarity; shorter series, which increase the available data, add noise. Hence the preference for annual series (Gligor & Ausloos, 2007: 139).

Unlike quantum mechanics, network analysis has become an integral component of the application of statistical mechanics to finance and economics. Its use includes mapping time series onto networks in order to analyse their global statistical properties – such as degree distributions, clustering coefficients and betweenness centrality (Dong et al., 2013: 270); studying persistence and correlation in time series by transforming them into complex textual networks (Karimi & Darooneh, 2013); and employing the Ising model to represent influential decision-making processes, allowing for heterogeneous interactions in which nodes do not exert equal influence on all their neighbours (Lucas, 2013).

Complex networks have also been used extensively to study sentiment contagion, first in the case of panic in financial markets (Zhao et al., 2014) and later in the context of market optimisation (Akyol & Alatas, 2020). Network analysis is now a tool in the econophysics study of market behaviour.

8 2018–2023: Measuring Uncertainty

The fourth phase, from 2018 to 2023, begins with a focus on behavioural aspects and market sentiment, which is not really the change of perspective it might appear. The focus on behavioural aspects, alongside quantum economics, network analysis and statistical mechanics more broadly, is integral to the identity of econophysics. Behavioural economics means decision-making, an aspect that takes on new importance in econophysics modelling, both in the definition of traditional variables such as financial asset prices and in relation to income distribution.

Partly as a result of individual choices and collective behaviour, the markets analysed seem to be characterised by increasing uncertainty and a greater need to measure this uncertainty, as it dominates the markets. Hence the recourse to the tools of econophysics to control and measure it. Some have called for institutional and political intervention, but only sporadically and in the field of distribution.

Market Sentiment

It could be asked how a discipline based on an analogy with mechanical statistics can strengthen the behavioural element, which by definition regards agents as decision-makers. Indeed, although immersed in the complexity of microscopic and macroscopic interactions at multiple spatial and temporal levels, econophysics ultimately takes account of behaviour.

Econophysics does not deny mechanical statistics and remains anchored to the primacy of the macroscopic level, interpreted in the light of microscopic dynamics. It changes the attitude towards the variables studied, be they prices, incomes, yields and so on, all of which are shrouded in uncertainty. This, together with the behavioural focus, is a strong feature of recent econophysics. Since nothing is predictable in the behaviour of economic and financial variables, nothing is mechanical. Behaviour and uncertainty overlap in a perspective in which the variables under consideration depend on the reactions, moods and feelings that ultimately make up the individuals acting in the markets.

The term 'sentiment' first appears in the dataset of articles used here in 2006 and becomes prevalent in 2013–2014, after which it is used extensively in line with in-depth studies of market characteristics that emphasise behavioural elements. For this reason, Jiri Kukacka and Joseph Barunik (2013: 5923) state that the most recent behavioural finance outcome employed by econophysics is market sentiment. The latter refers to exaggeratedly pessimistic or optimistic and, moreover, unrealistic beliefs about future market performance, securities cash flows and investment risks. These beliefs are not fully justified by the available information. Nevertheless, market sentiment seems to be one of the most powerful driving forces in the stock market. Therefore, more attention should be paid to the fact that decisions at the micro level are based on psychology and that biases can influence outcomes at the macro level.

The analysis of sentiment used as a proxy for expectations is facilitated by the wide availability of data on investors' reactions to changes in returns and prices

(Araújo et al., 2018). The study of investor sentiment is becoming central to the understanding of market fluctuations (Nguyen et al., 2023). The extreme volatility of cryptocurrencies seems inextricably linked to agents' sentiment (Javarone et al., 2023) or more broadly to market sentiment (Halperin, 2022), thereby embedding a new and significant relationship between micro- and macro-level perspectives, one that involves not only sentiment but also perception and cognitive evaluation.

Markets and Inequality

The discipline changes, but the links with the past remain. In 1906, Pareto wrote: 'It seems very likely, indeed almost certain, that humanitarian sentiments, legislative measures in favour of the poor, and other improvements in their condition contribute little or nothing to the increase of wealth, and sometimes even tend to reduce it' (Pareto, 1906: 204). Today we read that a 'fair' market cannot prevent inequality from growing, and that even equality of opportunity – without an explicit bias in favour of the rich – generates inequality (Cardoso et al., 2023). Although considered a necessary consequence of social and economic processes (Shaik, 2020), inequality is gaining prominence in the analysis of income distribution. An increasing number of models have been constructed to complement the analysis of exponential and power-law distributions, often used to explain the low and high portions of the Pareto curve, with agent-based approaches to account for the interaction between individuals (see Tian & Liu, 2020).

This has always been a hallmark of econophysics, and there is no doubt that at its current stage, starting with the distribution of income/wealth, its centre of gravity is the analysis of how local interactions between the components of a system determine complex macroscopic phenomena. But it is also true that the cognitive dimension of these components is no longer neglected.

Kinetic theory, as the oldest and most successful theory of many-body systems, has been widely developed in the context of income and wealth distribution in societies and was first applied to markets (Joseph & Chakrabarti, 2022). However, it now seems that further refinement is needed to take account of those forms of self-organisation which, in a context of competition or extreme competition, lead to greater inequality in the distribution of income. Indeed, while the Kolkata Institute's previously proposed a k-index for the Pareto distribution of 0.8 (80 per cent of wealth owned by 20 per cent of the population), the inequality k-index for the distribution in 2022 is 0.87 (87 per cent of wealth owned by 13 per cent of the population) (Manna et al., 2022). Increased competition shapes self-organising processes in a way that increases inequality. Similar breakpoints or k-indices characterise natural and social phenomena. It remains to be understood why increased competition leads to increased inequality, why it leads to a phase transition that further concentrates income and wealth.

In kinetic models, the total amount of money can be considered in the same way as the kinetic energy that characterises gas particles, with elastic collisions of molecules representing money exchange events between agents (Aydiner et al., 2018: 279). According to the prevailing economic interpretation, if we consider the distribution of wealth as a monetary distribution (Pascoal & Rocha, 2018), distributive inequality is the result of monetary exchange, with no other reason given than the 'creativity of these agents'. It can be shown that efficient markets lead to distributive inequality even if the individual growth rate has the same expected value for everyone, since risk increases or decreases individual growth above or below the average. This uncertainty increases the wealth gap between agents starting with similar wealth.

Hence, the need to represent both microscopic and macroscopic income and wealth distribution phenomena in a duality between subcritical and supercritical states, equivalent to that of the often-cited Ising model (Li & Boghosian, 2018). Couplings (exchanges) between neighbouring spins (individuals) are crucial to understand phase transitions, in both ferromagnetism and wealth distribution. Although essentially imitative, the microscopic behavioural dynamics are enriched compared to the original binary logic.

At the same time, the growing realisation that the market cannot be relied upon has led to the idea that mechanisms that favour the poorest, such as taxation and the redistribution of wealth, can guarantee a less unequal society (Cardoso et al., 2023: 4). Similarly, the redistribution of wealth can be accompanied by a certain number of social protections. Moreover, studying microscopic dynamics provides a better understanding of the level of risk (Neñer & Laguna, 2021), so that mitigation measures can be taken. In addition, an ownership-based model does not seem to reduce inequality; a tax-based model performs better (Fernandes & Tempere, 2020).

The reference to corrective political interventions only consolidates the interpretive framework of econophysics: the markets studied are characterised by quick decisions and the interactions of a multitude of subjects that do not require explanation, but description and representation, as precisely as possible, given the growing instability and uncertainty of the phenomena analysed. But they are also evidence of the individual and social perceptions of inequality that these market mechanisms determine.

Financial Markets and Entropy

It is interesting to note Bouchaud's observation that, given the impossibility of establishing why the prices of financial assets move, a model must be created to show how they move (2022: 79; see also Bouchaud & Potters, 2009). This wish is the essence of econophysics, active throughout the fourth phase, the first time econophysics focused on the why of price changes.

Financial markets have always been the core of econophysics, but after 2018 they became central, as shown by the positioning of 'stock markets' and 'investors'. The reception given to macroeconomics in the middle of the decade seems to be cooling, with the new interest in entropy coinciding with the spread of cryptocurrencies, discussed later.

Since its inception, entropy has been considered the most influential concept in statistical mechanics (Eddington, 1928), and its growth in relevance to econophysics has been gradual but steady, peaking around 2020–2021. It is well known that entropy can be a measure of disorder, a measure of ignorance of the system, or a measure of irreversible processes. In the context of information theory, entropy is a measure of the amount of uncertainty or randomness in a message (Shannon 1948; Debb, 2023). In econophysics, entropy is most commonly used as a measure of ignorance in stock and other financial markets, as reflected in references to entropy in Shannon (1948), Tsallis (2000) and Rényi (1961) (see Assaf et al., 2021). However, its relevance extends beyond this interpretation: entropy also possesses properties that make it a suitable measure of the uncertainty contained in a probability distribution (Ghosh et al., 2021). Finally, it often appears to be a measure of a kind of mixture of ignorance and disorder (Bentes & Menezes, 2012).

The aforementioned concepts of entropy originally arose in the context of studies of classical and quantum chaos, of physical systems far from equilibrium – think of turbulent systems and long-range interacting Hamiltonian systems. However, their application to the dynamics of financial markets has recently attracted considerable interest (Devi, 2017: 3). In particular, they have been used to test an assumption that characterises the traditional approach to financial market failure: the belief that extreme fluctuations are very rare. Hence the adoption of Tsallis's entropy (Tsallis, 2000), which is open to non-extensive statistical mechanics and can capture returns in fat-tailed distributions that allow for extreme fluctuations. Tsallis's entropy generalises the Boltzmann–Gibbs entropy by introducing an additional entropy index, q, whose non-linearity makes it well suited to capturing the non-linear phenomena commonly observed in stock market trading (see Ruiz & de Marcos, 2018). In particular, when dealing with the econophysics of heavy tails, unexpected events and non-equilibrium systems, reference to this notion of entropy prevails.

The reference to 'non-extensive statistical mechanics' is indicative of the fact that econophysics is emancipating itself from classical statistical mechanics in an attempt to provide an analysis of complex systems with long-range interactions and memory effects. The 'non-extensivity' coincides with the abandonment of the principle of linearity; entropy is no longer proportional to the size of the system. As a consequence, the additive Boltzmann–Gibbs entropy appears to be overcome in favour of a non-additive entropy suitable for complex, multifractal systems. As a result, long-range and large-scale correlations, multifractality and non-locality enter the lexicon of the discipline.

Stock/financial markets have remained central to economic physics, but with significant conceptual changes aimed at reshaping their properties. Suffice it to say that financial markets are now long memory, non-linear and multifractal. One could add the concept of transfer entropy to measure the transfer of information between different time series, even in different markets (Dimpfl & Peter, 2019; Xie et al., 2021) or to measure spillovers between cryptocurrencies (Huynh et al., 2020).

'Hysteresis' lies at the heart of Figure 1 around the year 2020. Hysteresis means that a system's subsequent state depends on its past history (Nicolis & Prigogine, 1989: 24). Hysteresis and memory effects are employed in a broad variety of fields and are particularly common in finance and economics (Cross, 1995). In economics, it is typically associated with the concepts of 'memory of shocks', 'multiple equilibria' and 'structural change' (Amable et al., 2004: 68). Examples of path dependence can be observed in labour market dynamics (Blanchard & Summers, 1986) and in international trade (Baldwin & Krugman, 1989). Risk aversion may persist after a financial crisis, reducing demand for credit and impeding economic recovery.

In econophysics, hysteresis is considered alongside bi-stability conditions. For example, in network analysis, strong economies of scale can result in multiple stable states and high transaction costs. This makes transitions between states discontinuous, leading to hysteresis (Schröder et al., 2018; Han et al., 2023). In conclusion, Arthur also emphasises the existence of built-in hysteresis: agents persist with their most plausible belief model, but abandon it when it becomes ineffective (Arthur, 2015: 165).

Interestingly, the idea of networks remains central, not least in helping to understand how information and/or 'disorder' is transferred from one market to another. The forecasting of financial asset prices, the ultimate goal of econophysics, faces market instability, and volatile markets, characterised by exceptional events, somehow become the norm. The study of volatile markets is crucial, with econophysics now placed as the discipline that deals with information and disorder entropy.

Finally, multi-scale Renyi's entropy is useful for studying entropy at the different scales at which asset returns can be expressed, in particular from cryptocurrencies to traditional assets such as gold, oil or equities (Lahmiri & Bekiros, 2020). Multi-scale entropy can be applied to study volatility on different time scales in order to understand the behaviour of asset prices and returns. If multi-scale entropy quantifies in time and space the complexity of time series of financial variables, multifractality – another key concept for the period – involves the breaking down of time series into multiple fractal components, each characterised by its own scaling exponents. Once the system has been defined in its complexity, its breakdown aids analysis.

The financial-stock-money market emerging in recent econophysics has little to do with the market of early econophysics. Disorder, memory, hysteresis, multifractality, to name but a few, have made it a new, more complex subject. The spread of cryptocurrencies has contributed to this.

Cryptocurrencies

'Multifractality' itself can have a significant behavioural component: the multifractal nature of financial time series, that is, collective behaviours based on emergent properties such as crises and speculation, determines volatility and similar-looking price changes in different time horizons. These phenomena are particularly evident in the affirmation of the cryptocurrency market.

Interest in cryptocurrencies is related to their returns, the study and prediction of which require tools that take into account the complexity of financial markets, characterised by variables that can behave differently over time. Multifractality is the mathematical tool that summarises this possibility. While stationarity implies the constancy of the mean and variance over time, multifractality allows for not one but a number of useful scaling exponents to describe different probability distributions and fluctuations. It can also be observed that multifractality is ubiquitously observable in both natural and complex socio-economic systems (Jiang et al., 2019). Therefore, the lack of stationarity typical of socio-economic phenomena is no longer an insurmountable obstacle to the application of cross-correlations or the analysis of long memory phenomena (Ghazani & Khosravi, 2020).

In financial economics, time-varying volatility is commonly used for option pricing, portfolio analysis and risk assessment. In econophysics, by contrast, volatility is of interest because of its power-law behaviour, which underlies phenomena such as extreme events, long-term memory and aftershock dynamics (see Kristoufek, 2013). The tendency is to use it in a relaxed version with a stable long tail, as in the Pareto distribution (Di Vita, 2020). Perturbations (shocks, crises) cause a relaxation of the distribution to which the system adapts by assuming a stable position. However, a relaxed state may be subject to further unpredictable perturbations.

Equipped with this conceptual and instrumental apparatus, econophysics is an appropriate tool for the study of cryptocurrencies, where extreme price volatility (especially in the years of the pandemic) makes them an attractive investment. The study of price volatility and information efficiency shows that market efficiency is an evolutionary rather than a stable phenomenon, and as such requires continuous measurement, hence entropy, albeit formulated as permutation entropy, remains central (Fernandes et al., 2022).

Competition among cryptocurrencies contributes to heightened price volatility. This effect is amplified by the absence of a central authority and by the greater susceptibility of these assets to media influence, which fuel speculation and volatility to a greater extent than in conventional currencies. As a result, there is an increased need to measure the entropy of the system (Stosic et al., 2019).

The market for bitcoins and cryptocurrencies, with multiple scaling behaviours and more complex patterns, involves a higher level of complexity than equity markets. If Brownian motion with constant mean and variance over time seemed sufficient to represent the movement of stock and option prices, cryptocurrency prices and returns require tools capable of accounting for multiple interacting scales, changing variances, heavy tails and skewness (Stosic et al., 2019). The use of 'wavelet analysis' to break down time series and identify those that are non-stationary, including by differentiating the scale and comparing series relating to different events, seems perfectly in line with an approach where the complexity of the phenomena analysed is an indispensable aspect (see Balcilar et al., 2022).

New in the final period analysed here is not so much the emergence of cryptocurrencies, albeit significant due to the market effects generated, as the consequence of these cryptocurrencies, in the context of evidently complex interactions at all levels, with increasing uncertainty regarding the variables analysed. Econophysics continues to be anchored in statistical mechanics, the object of study remains that of large aggregates, but an approach that dynamically combines macro and micro perspectives seems necessary for proper understanding (Li et al., 2022). Non-extensive statistical mechanics signifies this transformation, as does the widespread use of the concept of multifractality.

Interpretation of the macroscopic level and of all the related phenomena – processes of self-organisation, emergent properties, power-law distributions, multifractality, non-linear processes and so on – lies at the heart of econophysics.

However, the overview of these phenomena appears to be changing, not only the projection of these phenomena onto multiple spatial and temporal scales but also how to understand them – in other words, their cognitive dimension.

Conclusions

The story of econophysics does not end here. Anchoring economics and finance in mechanical statistics is an endeavour that is still in its infancy. But as it weaves its way through the many attempts of the twentieth century and establishes itself at the beginning of this century, this new field of research is showing the conceptual pillars on which it rests.

Having established that statistical mechanics deals with the macroscopic level, it can be said that none of the attempts to establish a socio-economic dimension, from Pareto/Bachelier to the econophysics of cryptocurrencies, places the individual, on the one hand, or a collective subject such as the state, on the other, at the centre of the analysis. Far from any individualistic ambitions, econophysics places the aggregate of elements at its centre. Not the aggregate as a monolithic subject but the aggregate as a set of exchanges between the subjects that make it up. Not the more or less rational individual or an institution such as the state but the interactions between individuals, between intermediate subjects, between states.

The study of aggregates has required the adaptation and refinement of tools from statistical mechanics, mathematics, biology and, of course, statistics. There are many examples: power laws, asymmetric distributions, the Ising model, the entanglement of quantum mechanics and other tools useful in the representation of relations among subjects, behaviours and sentiments. The market itself is grounded on interactions.

Interactions between individuals can result in stable distributions, giving rise to ordered and stable aggregates rather than disorder and chaos. This order results not necessarily from conscious behaviour but rather from processes of self-organisation and emergent coordination. Accordingly, skewed distributions cannot be attributed to a single cause but instead emerge from the complex interplay of multiple interactions between individuals. As markets are based on interactions, this perspective is central to the econophysics approach to studying them.

Econophysics tells us that interactions rather than decisions produce results: the many exchanges dominated by the heterogeneity of subjects, skills and interests that determine the unequal distribution of income are a good example of this. But the same can be said of the prices and/or yields of financial products.

This magmatic representation of the macroscopic level, grounded in aggregates of interactions, is facilitated by the absence in econophysics of an abstract benchmark – such as equilibrium – against which reality is to be compared. Instead, skewed distributions with more or less pronounced tails make it possible to capture economic relationships and phenomena in their stability and instability, their normality and exceptionality, within a single analytical framework. The focus thus remains on observed phenomena and their emergent properties, rather than on their conformity to an a priori theoretical construct.

Uncertainty has become a permanent feature of markets and interactions. This is a change to which econophysics has responded by measuring it and treating it as a constant. Interestingly, in attempting to measure uncertainty, but also to conceptualise it, econophysics has drawn on one of the founding concepts of statistical mechanics: entropy. A measure of thermal disorder in natural systems, entropy becomes a measure of uncertainty in economic and financial systems. Concepts such as uncertainty, entropy, self-organisation, emergent coordination and multifractality define a dynamic and complex reality – one that constitutes both the present focus of econophysics and its future trajectory.

References

Ahn, K., Choi, M. Y., Dai, B., Sohn, S. & Yang, B. (2017). Modeling stock return distributions with a quantum harmonic oscillator, *EPL* **120**, 38003.

Akyol, S. & Alatas, B. (2020). Sentiment classification within online social media using whale optimization algorithm and social impact theory-based optimization, *Physica A* **540**, 123094.

Alfi, V., Cristelli, M., Pietronero, L. & Zaccaria, A. (2009). Minimal agent-based model for financial markets I: Origin and self-organization of stylized facts, *The European Physical Journal B* **67**, 385–397.

Amable, B., Henry, J., Lordon, F. & Topol, R. (2004). Complex remanence vs. simple persistence: Are hysteresis and unit-root processes observationally equivalent? In W. A. Barnett, C. Deissenberg & G. Feichtinger (eds.), *Economic Complexity: Non-linear Dynamics, Multi-agents Economies, and Learning*, Amsterdam: Elsevier, 67–89.

Amoroso, L. (1924). La cinematica economica in un mercato chiuso. In R. Almagià (ed.), *Atti della Società Italiana per il Progresso delle Scienze*, Rome: SIPS, 1924, 137–163.

Amoroso, L. (1925). Ricerche intorno alla curva dei redditi, *Annali di matematica pura e applicata* **2**(1), 123–159.

Andersen, J. V. & Sornette, D. (2003). The $-game, *The European Physical Journal B* **31**, 141–145.

Angle, J. (2006). The inequality process as a wealth maximizing process, *Physica A* **367**, 388–414.

Anglin, P. M. (2005). Econophysics of wealth distribution: A comment. In A. Chatterjee, S. Yarlagadda & B. K. Chakrabarti (eds.), *Econophysics of Wealth Distributions*. Milan: Springer, 229–238.

Aoki, M. (1996). *New Approaches to Macroeconomic Modeling: Evolutionary Stochastic Dynamics, Multiple Equilibria, and Externalities as Field Effects*, Cambridge: Cambridge University Press.

Aoki, M. & Yoshikawa, H. (2007). *Reconstructing Macroeconomics: A Perspective from Statistical Physics and Combinatorial Stochastic Processes*, Cambridge: Cambridge University Press.

Aoyama, H., Fujiwara, Y., Ikeda, Y., Iyetomi, H., Souma, W. & Yoshokawa, Y. (2017). *Macro-econophysics: New Studies on Economic Networks and Synchronization*, Cambridge: Cambridge University Press.

Araújo, T., Eleutério, S. & Louçã, F. (2018). Do sentiments influence market dynamics? A reconstruction of the Brazilian stock market and its mood, *Physica A* **505**, 1139–1149.

Ardenghi, J. S. (2021). Quantum credit loans, *Physica A* **567**, 125656.

Ardenghi, J. S. (2023). Modeling amortization systems with vector spaces, *The European Physical Journal B* **96**, article 11.

Arthur, W. B. (1994). Inductive reasoning and bounded rationality, *American Economic Review* **84**(2), 406–411.

Arthur, W. B. (1999). Complexity and the economy, *Science* **284**, 107–109.

Arthur, W. B. (2015). *Complexity and the Economy*, Oxford: Oxford University Press.

Arthur, W. B., Durlauf, S. N. & Lane, D. A. (eds.) (1997). *The Economy as an Evolving Complex System II*, Reading, MA: Addison-Wesley.

Assaf, A., Bilgin, M. H. & Demir, E. (2021). Using transfer entropy to measure information flows between cryptocurrencies, *Physica A* **586**, 126484.

Auyang, S. Y. (1998). *Foundations of Complex-System Theories in Economics, Evolutionary Biology, and Statistical Physics*, Cambridge: Cambridge University Press.

Aydiner, E., Cherstvy, A. G. & Metzler, R. (2018). Wealth distribution, Pareto law, and stretched exponential decay of money: Computer simulations analysis of agent-based models, *Physica A* **490**, 278–288.

Bachelier, L. J. B. (1900). Théorie de la spéculation, *Annales scientifiques de l'É.N.S.* 3e série **17**, 21–86.

Bagarello, F. & Haven, E. (2015). Toward a formalization of a two traders' market with information exchange, *Physica Scripta* **90**, 015203.

Balcilar, M., Ozdemir, H. & Agan, B. (2022). Effects of Covid-19 on cryptocurrency and emerging market connectedness: Empirical evidence from quantile, frequency, and lasso networks, *Physica A* **604**, 127885.

Baldwin, R. & Krugman, P. (1989). Persistent effect of large exchange rate shocks, *Quarterly Journal of Economics* **4**, 635–654.

Banerjee, A. & Yakovenko, V. M. (2010). Universal patterns of inequality, *New Journal of Physics* **12**, 075032.

Bargigli, L. & Tedeschi, G. (2014). Interaction in agent-based economics: A survey on the network approach, *Physica A* **399**, 1–15.

Bassani, C. F. & the Council of the Italian Physical Society (CIPS) (eds.) (2006). *Ettore Majorana: Scientific Papers on Occasion of the Centary of His Birth*, Berlin: Springer.

Benhabib, J. & Bisin, A. (2018). Skewed wealth distributions: Theory and empirics, *Journal of Economic Literature* **56**(4), 1261–1291.

Bentes, S. R. & Menezes, R. (2012). Entropy: A new measure of stock market volatility? *Journal of Physics: Conference Series* **394**, 012033.

Berg, M., Hartley, B. & Richters, O. (2015). A stock-flow consistent input–output model with applications to energy price shocks, interest rates, and heat emissions, *New Journal of Physics* **17**, 015011.

Bernardelli, H. (1943). The stability of the income distribution, *Sankhyā: The Indian Journal of Statistics* **6**(4), 351–362.

Blanchard, O. & Summers, L. (1986). Hysteresis in unemployment. In S. Kirman (ed.), *NBER Macroeconomic Annual 1986*, Cambridge, MA: MIT Press, 15–78.

Bocci, C., Chiantini, L. & Rapallo, R. (2014). Max-plus objects to study the complexity of graphs, *Methodology and Computing in Applied Probability* **16**, 507–525.

Bouchaud, J.-P. (2001). Power laws in economics and finance: Some ideas from physics, *Quantitative Finance* **1**, 105–112.

Bouchaud, J.-P. (2022). Radical complexity. In R. Kutner, C. Schinckus & H. E. Stanley (eds.), Three Risky Decades: A Time for Econophysics? Special Issue, *Entropy* **24**, 79–88.

Bouchaud, J.-P. & Potters, M. (2009). *Theory of Financial Risk and Derivative Pricing: From Statistical Physics to Risk Management*, Cambridge: Cambridge University Press.

Brandouy, O., Corelli, A., Veryzhenko, I. & Waldeck R. (2012). A re-examination of the 'zero is enough' hypothesis in the emergence of financial stylized facts, *Journal of Economic Interaction and Coordination* **7**, 223–248.

Cajueiro, D. S. & Soares De Camargo, R. (2006). Minority game with local interactions due to the presence of herding behavior, *Physica A* **355**, 280–284.

Cantelli, F. P. (1921). Sulla deduzione delle leggi di frequenza da considerazioni di probabilità, *Metron* **2**(3), 83–91.

Cantelli, F. P. (1929). Sulla legge di distribuzione dei redditi, *Giornale degli Economisti e Rivista di Statistica* **69**(11), 850–852.

Cardoso, B.-H. F., Gonçalves, S. & Iglesias, J. R. (2023). Why equal opportunities lead to maximum inequality? The wealth condensation paradox generally solved, *Chaos, Solitons and Fractals* **168**(C), 113181.

Casdagli, M. & Eubank, S. (eds.) (1990). *Nonlinear Modeling and Forecasting*, Redwood City, CA: Addison-Wesley.

Castellani, M. (1950). On multinomial distributions with limited freedom: A stochastic genesis of Pareto's and Pearson's curves, *Annals of Mathematical Statistics* **21**, 289–93.

Castelnuovo, G. (1919). *Calcolo delle Probabilità*, Milan: Società Editrice Dante Alighieri.

Chakrabarti, B. K. (2005). Econophysics-Kolkata: A short story. In A. Chatterjee, S. Yarlagadda & B. K. Chakrabarti (eds.), *Econophysics of Wealth Distributions*. Milan: Springer, 225–228.

Chakrabarti, B. K. (2018). Econophysics as conceived by Meghnad Saha, *Science and Culture* **84**, 365–369.

Chakrabarti, B. K., Chakraborti, A. & Chatterjee, A. (eds.) (2006). *Econophysics and Sociophysics*, Weinheim: Wiley.

Chakrabarti, B. K. & Sinha, A. (2021). Development of econophysics: A biased account and perspective from Kolkata, *Entropy* **23**, 254.

Challet, D., Marsili, M. & Zhang, I.-C. (2001). Minority games and stylized facts, *Physica A* **299**(1–2), 228–233.

Champernowne, D. G. (1953). A model of income distribution, *Economic Journal* **63**(250), 318–351.

Chatterjee, A. (2009). Kinetic models for wealth exchange on directed networks, *The European Physical Journal B* **67**, 593–598.

Chatterjee, A. & Chakrabarti, B. K. (2007). Kinetic exchange models for income and wealth distributions, *The European Physical Journal B* **60**, 135–149.

Chatterjee, A., Chakrabarti, B. K. & Manna, S. S. (2003). Money in gas-like markets: Gibbs and Pareto laws, *Physica Scripta* **T106**, 36–38.

Chatterjee, A., Chakrabarti, B. K. & Manna, S. S. (2004). Pareto law in a kinetic model of market with random saving propensity, *Physica A* **335**, 155–163.

Chatterjee, A. & Sen, P. (2010). Agent dynamics in kinetic models of wealth exchange, *Physical Review E* **82**, 1–6.

Chen, S.-H. & Li, S.-P. (2012). Econophysics: Bridges over a turbulent current, *International Review of Financial Analysis* **23**, 1–10.

Clementi, F., Di Matteo, T., Gallegati, M. & Kaniadakis, G. (2008). The κ-generalized distribution: A new descriptive model for the size distribution of incomes, *Physics A* **387**, 3201–3208.

Clementi, F. & Gallegati, M. (2016). *The Distribution of Income and Wealth: Parametric Modeling with the κ-Generalized Family*, Berlin: Springer.

Clementi, F., Gallegati, M. & Kaniadakis, G. (2007). κ-generalized statistics in personal income distribution, *The European Physical Journal B* **57**, 187–193.

Cockshott, W. P., Cottrell, A. F., Michaelson, G. J., Wright, I. P. & Yakovenko, V. M. (2009). *Classical Econophysics*, London: Routledge.

Cootner, P. H. (1964). *The Random Character of Stock Market Prices*, Cambridge, MA: MIT Press.

Costantini, D. (2004). *I fondamenti storico-filosofici delle discipline statistico-probabilistiche*, Turin: Bollati Boringhieri.

Cross, R. (1995). Metaphors and time reversibility and irreversibility in economic systems, *Journal of Economic Methodology* **2**(1), 123–134.

Da Silva Junior, L. C. & de Figueirêdo, P. H. (2014). Income distribution: An adaptive heterogeneous model, *Physica A* **395**, 275–282.

Debb, O. E. (2023). Entropic spatial auto-correlation of voter uncertainty and voter transitions in parliamentary elections, *Physica A* **617**, 128675.

Delli Gatti, D., Di Guilmi, C., Gaffeo, E. & Gallegati, M. (2004). Bankruptcy as an exit mechanism for systems with a variable number of components, *Physica A* **344**, 8–13.

De Martino, A. & Marsili, M. (2006). Statistical mechanics of socio-economic systems with heterogeneous agents, *Journal of Physics A: Mathematical and General* **39**, R465.

Devi, S. (2017). Financial market dynamics: Superdiffusive or not? *Journal of Statistical Mechanics: Theory and Experiment* 083207.

Di Matteo, T., Pozzi, F. & Aste, T. (2010). The use of dynamical networks to detect the hierarchical organization of financial market sectors, *The European Physical Journal B* **73**, 3–11.

Dimpfl, T. & Peter, F. J. (2019). Group transfer entropy with an application to cryptocurrencies, *Physica A* **516**, 543–551.

Ding, N., Xi, N. & Wang, Y. (2003). Effects of saving and spending patterns on holding time distribution, *The European Physical Journal B* **36**, 149–153.

Dirac, P. A. M. (1935). *The Principles of Quantum Mechanics*, Oxford: Clarendon Press.

Di Vita, A. (2020). On avalanche-like perturbations of relaxed power-law distributions: Richardson's law of warfare as a consequence of the relaxation to a Pareto-like distribution of wealth, *The European Physical Journal B* **93**, 27.

Djauhari, M. A. & Gan, S. L. (2015). Optimality problem of network topology in stocks market analysis, *Physica A* **419**, 108–114.

Djauhari, M. A. & Gan, S. L. (2016). Network topology of economic sectors, *Journal of Statistical Mechanics: Theory and Experiment* 093401.

Dong, Y., Huang, W., Liu, Z. & Guan, S. (2013). Network analysis of time series under the constraint of fixed nearest neighbors, *Physica A* **392**, 967–973.

Dragulescu, A. & Yakovenko, V. M. (2000). Statistical mechanics of money, *The European Physical Journal B* **17**, 723–729.

Düring, B., Matthes, D. & Toscani, G. (2008). Kinetic equations modelling wealth redistribution: A comparison of approaches, *Physical Review E* **78**, 056103.

Eddington, A. S. (1928). *The Nature of the Physical World*, New York: Macmillan.

Ehrenfest, P. & Ehrenfest, T. (1990). *The Conceptual Foundations of the Statistical Approach in Mechanics*, New York: Dover.

Fagiolo, G. (2010). The international-trade network: Gravity equations and topological properties, *Journal of Economic Interaction and Coordination* **5**, 1–25.

Fagiolo, G. & Valente, M. (2005). Minority games, local interactions, and endogenous networks, *Computational Economics* **25**, 41–57.

Farjoun, E. & Machover, M. (1983). *Laws of Chaos: A Probabilistic Approach to Political Economy*, London: Verso.

Fernandes, L. & Tempere, J. (2020). Effect of segregation on inequality in kinetic models of wealth exchange, *The European Physical Journal B* **93**, 37.

Fernandes, L. H. S., Bouri, E., Silva, J. W. L., Bejan, L. & de Araujo, F. H. A. (2022). The resilience of cryptocurrency market efficiency to Covid-19 shock, *Physica A* **607**, 128218.

Ferreira, F. F., de Oliveira, V. M., Crepaldi, A. F. & Campos, P. R. A. (2005). Agent-based model with heterogeneous fundamental prices, *Physica A* **357**, 534–542.

Foley, D. K. (2003). Statistical equilibrium in economics: Method, interpretation, and an example. In F. Petri & F. Hahn (eds.), *General Equilibrium: Problems and Prospects*, London: Routledge, 95–116.

Föllmer, H. (1974). Random economies with many interactive agents, *Journal of Mathematical Economics* **1**, 51–62.

Franke, F. & Asada, T. (2008). Incorporating positions into asset pricing models with order-based strategies, *Journal of Economic Interaction and Coordination* **3**, 201–227.

Fujiwara, Y., Di Guilmi, C., Aoyama, H., Gallegati, M., & Souma, M. (2004). Do Pareto–Zipf and Gibrat laws hold true? An analysis with European firms, *Physica A* **335**, 197–216.

Gabaix, X. (2009). Power laws in economics and finance, *Annual Review of Economics* **1**, 255–293.

Gabaix, X. (2016). Power laws in economics: An introduction, *Journal of Economic Perspectives* **30**(1), 185–206.

Galla, T., Coolen, A. C. C. & Sherrington, D. (2003). Dynamics of a spherical minority game, *Journal of Physics A: Mathematical and General* **36**(43), 11159–11172.

Gallegati, M. (2016). Beyond econophysics (not to mention mainstream economics), *The European Physical Journal Special Topic* **225**, 3179–3185.

Gallegati, M., Keen, S., Lux, T. & Ormerod, P. (2006). Worrying trends in econophysics, *Physica A* **370**, 1–6.

Gallegati, M. & Kirman, A. (eds.) (1999). *Beyond the Representative Agent*, Cheltenham: Edward Elgar.

Gallegati, M. & Kirman, A. (2019). 20 years of WEHIA: A journey in search of a safer road, *Journal of Economic Behavior and Organization* **157**, 5–14.

Galstyan, A. & Lerman, K. (2002). Minority games and distributed coordination in non- stationary environments, *Proceedings of the 2002 International Joint Conference on Neural Networks* **3**, 2610–2614.

Garas, A., Schweitzer, F. & Havlin, S. (2012). A k-shell decomposition method for weighted networks, *New Journal of Physics* **14**, 083030.

Garibaldi, U. & Scalas, E. (2010). *Finitary Probabilistic Methods in Econophysics*, Cambridge: Cambridge University Press.

Genthon, H. (2020). The concept of velocity in the history of Brownian motion, *The European Physical Journal H* **45**, 49–105.

Ghazani, M. M. & Khosravi, R. (2020). Multifractal detrended cross-correlation analysis on benchmark cryptocurrencies and crude oil prices, *Physica A* **560**, 125172.

Ghosh, A., Shreya, P. & Basu, B. (2021). Maximum entropy framework for a universal rank order distribution with socio-economic applications, *Physica A* **563**, 125433.

Giardina, I. & Bouchaud, J.-P. (2003). Bubbles, crashes and intermittency in agent based market models, *The European Physical Journal B* **31**, 421–437.

Gibbs, J. W. (1914). *Elementary Principles in Statistical Mechanics, Developed with Special Reference to the Rational Foundations of Thermodynamics*, New Haven, CT: Yale University Press.

Gibrat, R. (1931). *Les inégalités économiques*, Paris: Sire.

Gilmore, C. G., Lucey, B. M. & Boscia, M. (2008). An ever-closer union? Examining the evolution of linkages of European equity markets via minimum spanning trees, *Physica A* **387**(25), 6319–6329.

Gligor, M. & Ausloos, M. (2007). Cluster structure of EU-15 countries derived from the correlation matrix analysis of macroeconomic index fluctuations, *The European Physical Journal B* **57**, 139–146.

Gligor, M. & Ignat, M. (2002). A kinetic approach to some quasi-linear laws of macroeconomics, *The European Physical Journal B* **30**, 125–135.

Górski, A. Z., Drożdż, S. & Speth, J. (2002). Financial multifractality and its subtleties: An example of DAX. *Physica A* **136**(1–4), 496–510.

Grau-Carles, P. (2000). Empirical evidence of long-range correlations in stock returns, *Physica A* **287**(3–4), 396–404.

Greenacre, M. (2007). *Correspondence Analysis in Practice*, Boca Raton, FL: Chapman & Hall.

Halperin, I. (2022). Non-equilibrium skewness, market crises, and option pricing: Non-linear Langevin model of markets with supersymmetry, *Physica A* **594**, 127065.

Han, C., Schröder, M., Witthaut, D. & Böttcher, P. C. (2023). Formation of trade networks by economies of scale and product differentiation, *Journal of Physics: Complexity* **4**, 025006.

Harman, P. (1998). *The Natural Philosophy of James Clerk Maxwell*, Cambridge: Cambridge University Press.

Heimel, J. A. F. & De Martino, A. (2001). Broken ergodicity and memory in the minority game, *Journal of Physics A: Mathematical and General* **34**, L539–L545.

Helbing, D. (2003). Modelling supply networks and business cycles as unstable transport phenomena, *New Journal of Physics* **5**, 90.

Huynh, T. L. D., Nasir, M. A., Vo, X. V. & Nguyen, T. T. (2020). 'Small things matter most': The spillover effects in the cryptocurrency market and gold as a silver bullet, *North American Journal of Economics and Finance* **54**, 101277.

Ikeda, Y., Souma, W., Aoyama, H., Iyetomi, H., Fujiwara, Y. & Kaizoji, T. (2007). Quantitative agent-based firm dynamics simulation with parameters estimated by financial and transaction data analysis, *Physica A* **375**(2), 651–667.

Iqbal, A., Chappell, J. M. & Abbott, D. (2015). Social optimality in quantum Bayesian games, *Physica A* **436**, 798–805.

Ivanov, P. C., Podobnik, B., Lee, Y. & Stanley, H. E. (2001). Truncated Lévy process with scale-invariant behavior, *Physica A* **299**, 154–160.

Jain, S. & Buckley, P. (2006). Persistence in financial markets, *The European Physical Journal B* **50**, 133–136.

Javarone, M. A., Di Antonio, G., Vinci, G. V., Cristodaro, R., Tessone, C. J. & Pietronero, L. (2023). Disorder unleashes panic in bitcoin dynamics. *Journal of Physics: Complexity* **4**, 045002.

Jaynes, E. T. (2003). *Probability Theory: The Logic of Science*, Cambridge: Cambridge University Press.

Jiang, Z.-Q., Xie, W.-J., Zhou, W.-X. & Sornette, D. (2019). Multifractal analysis of financial markets: A review, *Report on Progress in Physics* **82**, 125901.

Joseph, B. & Chakrabarti, B. K. (2022). Variation of Gini and Kolkata indices with saving propensity in the kinetic exchange model of wealth distribution: An analytical study, *Physica A* **594**, 127051.

Jovanovic, F. & Schinckus, C. (2017). *Econophysics and Financial Economics: An Emerging Dialogue*, Oxford: Oxford University Press.

Karimi, S. & Darooneh, A. H. (2013). Measuring persistence in a stationary time series using the complex network theory, *Physica A* **392**(1), 287–293.

Kocakaplan, Y., Deviren, B. & Keskin, M. (2012). Hierarchical structures of correlations networks among Turkey's exports and imports by currencies, *Physica A* **391**(24), 6509–6518.

Kristoufek, L. (2013). Testing power-law cross-correlations: Rescaled covariance test, *The European Physical Journal B* **86**, 418.

Kristoufek, L. (2014). Measuring correlations between non-stationary series with DCCA coefficient, *Physica A* **402**, 291–298.

Krüger, L. (1990). The probabilistic revolution in physics: An overview. In L. Krüger, G. Gigerenzer & M. S. Morgan (eds.), *The Probabilistic Revolution*, vol. II, Cambridge, MA: MIT Press, 374–378.

Krüger, L., Gigerenzer, G. & Morgan, M. S. (eds.) (1990). *The Probabilistic Revolution, Volume II: Ideas in the Sciences*, Cambridge, MA: MIT Press.

Kukacka, J. & Barunik, J. (2013). Behavioural breaks in the heterogeneous agent model: The impact of herding, overconfidence, and market sentiment, *Physica A* **392**, 5920–5938.

Lahmiri, S. & Bekiros, S. (2020). Renyi entropy and mutual information measurement of market expectations and investor fear during the Covid-19 pandemic, *Chaos, Solitons and Fractals* **139**, 110084.

Lévy, P. (1925). *Calcul des probabilités*, Paris: Gauthier-Villars.

Lévy, P. (1937–1954). *Théorie de l'addition des variables aléatoires*, Paris: Gauthier-Villars.

Lévy, P. (1948–1965). *Processus stochastiques et mouvement brownien*, Paris: Gauthier-Villars.

Li, J. & Boghosian, B. M. (2018). Duality in an asset exchange model for wealth distribution, *Physica A* **497**, 154–165.

Li, J.-C., Tao, C. & Li, H.-F. (2022). Dynamic forecasting performance and liquidity evaluation of financial market by econophysics and Bayesian methods, *Physica A* **588**, 126546.

Lillo, F. & Mantegna, R. N. (2000). Symmetry alteration of ensemble return distribution in crash and rally days of financial markets, *The European Physical Journal B* **15**, 603–606.

Lisman, J. (1949). *Econometrics, Statistics and Thermodynamics*, The Hague: Netherlands Postal and Telephone Services.

Lucas, A. (2013). Binary decision making with very heterogeneous influence, *Journal of Statistical Mechanics* P09024.

Lux, T. & Alfarano, S. (2016). Financial power laws: Empirical evidence, models, and mechanisms, *Chaos, Solitons and Fractals* **88**, 3–18.

Majorana, E. (1942). Il valore delle leggi statistiche nella fisica e nelle scienze sociali, *Scientia* **71**, 58–66. English edition: The value of statistical laws in physics and social sciences, *Ettore Majorana Scientific Papers*, ed. F. Bassani et al., trans. R. Mantegna, 2006. Bologna: SIF and Springer.

Malcai, O., Biham, O., Richmond, P. & Solomon, S. (2002). Theoretical analysis and simulations of the generalized Lotka-Volterra model, *Physical Review E* **66**, 031102.

Mandelbrot, B. B. (1960). The Pareto-Lévy law and the distribution of income, *International Economic Review* **1**(2), 79–106.

Mandelbrot, B. B. (1963a). New methods in statistical economics, *Journal of Political Economy* **71**(5), 421–440.

Mandelbrot, B. B. (1963b). The variation of certain speculative prices, *Journal of Business* **36**(4), 394–419.

Mandelbrot, B. B. (1963c). The stable Paretian income distribution when the apparent exponent is near two, *International Economic Review* **4**(1), 111–115.

Mandelbrot, B. B. (2009). New methods of statistical economics, revisited: Short versus long tails and Gaussian versus power-law distributions, *Complexity* **14**(3), 55–65.

Manna, S. S., Biswas, S. & Chakrabarti, B. K. (2022). Near universal values of social inequality indices in self-organized critical models, *Physica A* **596**, 127121.

Mantegna, R. N. (1999). Hierarchical structures in financial markets, *The European Physical Journal B* **11**, 193–197.

Mantegna, R. N. & Stanley, H. E. (2000). *An Introduction to Econophysics: Correlations and Complexity in Economics*, Cambridge: Cambridge University Press.

Marschinski, R. & Kantz, V. (2002). Analysing the information flow between financial time series: An improved estimator for transfer entropy, *The European Physical Journal B* **30**, 275–281.

McCauley, J. L. (2007). Response to worrying trends in econophysics, *MPRA Paper No. 2129*.

McCauley, J. L., Roehner, B., Stanley, H. E. & Schinckus, C. (2016). Editorial: The 20th anniversary of econophysics: Where we are and where we are going, *International Review of Financial Analysis* **47**, 267–269.

Ménard, C. (1990). Why was there no probabilistic revolution in economic thought? In L. Krüger, G. Gigerenzer & M. S. Morgan (eds.), *The Probabilistic Revolution*. Cambridge, MA: MIT Press, 139–146.

Meng, X., Zhang, J.-W., Xu, J. & Guo, H. (2015). Quantum spatial-periodic harmonic model for daily price-limited stock markets, *Physica A* **438**, 154–160.

Miccichè, S. (2013). Empirical relationship between stocks' cross-correlation and stocks' volatility clustering, *Journal of Statistical Mechanics* P05015.

Mirowski, P. (1989). *More Heat Than Light: Economics as Social Physics, Physics as Nature's Economics*, Cambridge: Cambridge University Press.

Mirowski, P. (1990). From Mandelbrot to chaos in economic theory, *Southern Economic Journal* **57**(2), 289–307.

Morgan, M. S. (1990). Statistics without probability in econometrics. In L. Krüger, G. Gigerenzer & M. S. Morgan (eds.), *The Probabilistic Revolution*, Cambridge, MA: MIT Press, 171–197.

Morgan, M. S. (2012). *The World in the Model*, Cambridge: Cambridge University Press.

Moukarzel, C. F. (2013). Per-capita GDP and nonequilibrium wealth-concentration in a model for trade, *Journal of Physics: Conference Series* **475**, 012011.

Musciotto, F., Marotta, L., Miccichè, S., Piilo, J. & Mantegna, R. N. (2016). Patterns of trading profiles at the Nordic stock exchange: A correlation-based approach, *Chaos, Solitons and Fractals* **88**, 267–278.

Neñer, J. & Laguna, M. F. (2021). Optimal risk in wealth exchange models: Agent dynamics from a microscopic perspective, *Physica A* **566**, 125625.

Newman, M. (2005). Power laws, Pareto distribution and Zipf's law, *Contemporary Physics* **46**(5), 323–351.

Nguyen, A. P. N., Mai, T. T., Bezbradica, M. & Crane, M. (2023). Volatility and returns connectedness in cryptocurrency markets: Insights from graph-based methods, *Physica A* **632**, 129349.

Nicolis, G. & Prigogine, I. (1989). *Exploring Complexity*, New York: Freeman and Co.

Ormerod, P. (2016). Ten years after 'worrying trends in econophysics': Developments and current challenges, *The European Physical Journal Special Topics* **225**, 3281–3291.

Orrell, D. (2020). *Quantum Economics and Finance: An Applied Mathematics Introduction*, New York: Panda Ohana.

Osborne, M. F. M. (1964). Periodic structure in the Brownian motion of stock prices. In P. H. Cootner (ed.), *The Random Character of Stock Market Prices*, Cambridge, MA: MIT Press, 262–296.

Pareto, V. (1896–1897). *Cours d'Economie Politique*. Genève: Droz. New edition ed. G. H. Bousquet & G. Busino, 1964.

Pareto, V. (1906). *Manuale di Economia Politica*. English edition: *Manual of Political Economy*, ed. A. Montesano, A. Zanni, L. Bruni, J. C. Chipman & M. McLure, 2014. Oxford: Oxford University Press.

Pareto, V. (1916). *Trattato di Sociologia Generale*, 3 vols. English edition: *The Mind and Society: A Treatise on General Sociology*, 2 vols., ed. V. Pareto, 1935. New York: Dover.

Pareto, V. (1922). Previsione dei Fenomeni Economici. Reprinted in *Écrits Sociologiques Mineurs*, ed. G. Busino, 1980. Geneva: Droz.

Pascoal, R. & Rocha, H. (2018). Inequality measures for wealth distribution: Population vs individual perspective, *Physica A* **492**, 1317–1326.

Patriarca, M., Heinsalu, E. & Chakraborti, A. (2010). Basic kinetic wealth-exchange models: Common features and open problems, *The European Physical Journal B* **73**, 145–153.

Pawela, L. (2016). Quantum games on evolving random networks, *Physica A* **458**, 179–188.

Petracca, E. (2019). The rejection of Andrew G. Pikler from postwar American economics, *European Journal of the History of Economic Thought* **26**(3), 554–586.

Pikler, A. (1951). The Quanta-kinetic model of the monetary theory, *Metroeconomica* **3**(2), 70–95.

Plerou, V., Gopikrishnan, P., Rosenow, B., Amaral, L. A. N. & Stanley, H. E. (2000). Econophysics: Financial time series from a statistical physics point of view, *Physica A* **279**, 443–456.

Rényi, A. (1961). On measures of entropy and information. In J. Neyman (ed.), *Proceedings of the Fourth Berkeley Symposium on Mathematical Statistics and Probability, Volume 1: Contributions to the Theory of Statistics*. Berkeley: University of California Press, 547–561.

Richmond, P., Sexton, M. B., Hardiman, S. J. & Hutzler, S. (2014). Generalised diffusion model of asset price fluctuations, *The European Physical Journal B* **87**, 63.

Roehner, B. M. (2008). Econophysics: Challenges and promises – An observation-based approach, *Evolutionary Institutional Economic Review* **4**(2), 251–266.

Ruiz, G. & de Marcos, A. F. (2018). Evidence for criticality in financial data, *The European Physical Journal B* **91**, 1.

Schröder, M., Nagler, J., Timme, M. & Witthaut, D. (2018). Hysteretic percolation from locally optimal individual decisions, *Physical Review Letters* **120**, 248302.

Schweitzer, F. (2003). *Brownian Agents and Active Particles*, Berlin: Springer.

Sethna, J. P. (2021). *Statistical Mechanics: Entropy, Order Parameters, and Complexity*, Oxford: Oxford University Press.

Shaikh, A. (2020). The econ in econophysics, *The European Physical Journal Special Topics* **229**, 1675–1684.

Shaikh, A., Papanikolaou, N. & Wiener, N. (2014). Race, gender and the econophysics of income distribution in the USA, *Physica A* **415**, 54–60.

Shannon, C. E. (1948). A mathematical theory of communication, *Bell System Technical Journal* **27**, 379–423, 623–665.

Shubik, M. & Smith, E. (2009). Econophysics: Present and future, *Complexity* **14**(3), 9–10.

Slanina, F. (2014). *Essentials of Econophysics Modelling*, Oxford: Oxford University Press.

Sornette, D. (2002). 'Slimming' of power-law tails by increasing market returns, *Physica A* **309**(3–4), 403–418.

Sornette, D. (2014). Physics and financial economics (1776–2014): Puzzles, Ising and agent-based models, *Reports on Progress in Physics* **77**, 062001.

Stanley, H. E., Amaral, L. A. N., Gopikrishnan, P., Plerou, V. & Salinger, M. A. (2002). Scale invariance and universality in economic phenomena, *Journal of Physics: Condensed Matter* **14**, 2121–2131.

Stanley, H. E., Gabaix, X., Gopikrishnan, P. & Plerou, V. (2007). Economic fluctuations and statistical physics: Quantifying extremely rare and less rare events in finance, *Physica A* **382**, 286–301.

Stanley, H. E., Nunes Amaral, L. A., Gabaix, X., Gopikrishnan, P. & Plerou, V. (2001). Quantifying economic fluctuations, *Physica A* **302**, 126–137.

Steindl, J. (1965). *Random Process and the Growth of Firms: A Study of the Pareto Law*, Vienna: Griffin & Co.

Stosic, Da., Stosic, Du., Ludermir, T. B. & Stosic, T. (2019). Exploring disorder and complexity in the cryptocurrency space, *Physica A* **525**, 548–556.

Tian, S. & Liu, Z. (2020). Emergence of income inequality: Origin, distribution and possible policies, *Physica A* **537**, 122767.

Toth, B., Kertész, J. & Farmer, J. D. (2009). Studies of the limit order book around large price changes, *The European Physical Journal B* **71**, 499–510.

Tsallis, C. (2000). *Introduction to Nonextensive Statistical Mechanics*, New York: Springer.

Tsirlin, A. M., Kazakov, V. & Kolinko, N. A. (2003). A minimal dissipation type-based classification in irreversible thermodynamics and microeconomics, *The European Physical Journal B* **35**, 565–570.

Tusset, G. (2018). *From Galileo to Modern Economics: The Italian Origins of Econophysics*, Cham: Springer.

Vinci, F. (1921). Nuovi contributi allo studio della distribuzione dei redditi, *Giornale degli economisti e Rivista di Statistica* **61**(11), 365–369.

Vinci, F. (1924). Calcolo delle probabilità e distribuzione dei redditi nel pensiero di Pareto, *Giornale degli economisti e Rivista di Statistica* **64**(1/2), 127–129.

Wang, B. H. & Hui, P. M. (2001). The distribution and scaling of fluctuations for Hang Seng index in Hong Kong stock market, *The European Physical Journal B* **20**, 573–579.

Weigend, A. & Gershenfeld, N. (eds.) (1994). *Time Series Prediction: Forecasting the Future and Understanding the Past*, Redwood City, CA: Addison-Wesley.

Wiener, N. (1921). The average of an analytic functional and the Brownian movement, *Proceedings of the National Academy of Sciences* **7**, 294–298.

Xie, W.-J., Yong, Y., Wei, N., Yue, P. & Zhou, W.-X. (2021). Identifying states of global financial market based on information flow network motifs, *North American Journal of Economics and Finance* **58**, 101459.

Xie, W.-J., Jiang, Z.-Q., Gu, G.-F., Xiong, X. & Zhou, W.-X. (2015). Joint multifractal analysis based on the partition function approach: Analytical analysis, numerical simulation, and empirical application, *New Journal of Physics* **17**, 103020.

Yakovenko, V. M. (2016). Monetary economics from econophysics perspective, *The European Physical Journal B* **225**, 3313–3335.

Yakovenko, V. M. & Rosser Jr, J. B. (2009). Colloquium: Statistical mechanics of money, wealth, and income, *Review of Modern Physics* **81**, 1703–1725.

Yang, C.-B. & Cai, X. (2002). A possible origin of power-law distribution in stock markets, *Chinese Physics Letters* **19**, 772.

Yegorov, Y. (2007). Econophysics: A perspective of matching two sciences, *Evolutionary Institutional Economic Review* **4**(1), 143–170.

Yukalov, V. I. & Sornette, D. (2015). Quantum theory of measurements as quantum decision theory, *Journal of Physics: Conference Series* **594**, 012048.

Yukalov, V. I. & Sornette, D. (2016a). Inconclusive quantum measurements and decisions under uncertainty, *Frontiers in Physics* **4**, 1–9.

Yukalov, V. I. & Sornette, D. (2016b). Quantum probability and quantum decision-making, *Philosophical Transactions A* **374**, 20150100.

Yukalov, V. I. & Sornette, D. (2017). Quantum probabilities as behavioral probabilities, *Entropy* **19**, 12.

Yukalov, V. I., Yukalova, E. P. & Sornette, D. (2018). Information processing by networks of quantum decision makers, *Physica A* **492**, 747–766.

Zabaleta, O. G., Barrangù, J. P. & Arizmendi, C. M. (2017). Quantum game application to spectrum scarcity problems, *Physica A* **466**, 455–461.

Zanin, M., Papo, P., Romance, M., Criado, R. & Moral, S. (2016). The topology of card transaction money flows, *Physica A* **462**, 134–140.

Zhao, L., Wang, J., Huang, R., Cui, H., Qiu, X. & Wang, X. (2014). Sentiment contagion in complex networks, *Physica A* **394**, 17–23.

Zhou, J., Gu, G.-F., Jiang, Z.-Q., Xiong, X., Chen, W., Zhang, W. & Zhou, W.-X. (2017). Computational experiments successfully predict the emergence of autocorrelations in ultra-high-frequency stock returns, *Computational Economics* **50**, 579–594.

Zurek, W. H. (ed.) (1989). *Complexity, Entropy, and the Physics of Information*, Redwood City, CA: Addison-Wesley.

Acknowledgements

We thank the Italian Ministry of University and Research for PRIN funding – Progetti di Ricerca di Rilevante Interesse Nazionale (Research Projects of Significant National Interest) – reference number 2020X24S9N_002.

Cambridge Elements

Econophysics

Series Editors

Rosario Nunzio Mantegna
University of Palermo

Rosario Nunzio Mantegna is Professor of Applied Physics at the University of Palermo and an external faculty member of the Complexity Science Hub in Vienna. He is one of the pioneers of econophysics and economic networks, and he co-authored the first book on the topic ('Introduction to Econophysics', Cambridge, 1999).

Bikas K. Chakrabarti
Saha Institute of Nuclear Physics

Bikas K. Chakrabarti is Emeritus Professor at Saha Institute of Nuclear Physics and visiting Professor of Economics in the Indian Statistical Institute, Kolkata. He has co-authored more than two hundred papers and ten books (including 'Econophysics of Income & Wealth Distributions', Cambridge, 2013). In 1995, he organized a conference in Kolkata, where the term "econophysics" was first coined.

Mauro Gallegati
Polytechnic University of Marche, Ancona

Mauro Gallegati is Professor of Economics at Polytechnic University of Marche, Ancona. He has previously held visiting scholarships at Cambridge, Stanford, MIT, Columbia, the Santa Fe Institute, the Brookings Institution, and ETH Zurich. His research includes business fluctuations, nonlinear dynamics, models of financial fragility, and heterogeneous interacting agents.

Irena Vodenska
Boston University

Irena Vodenska is Professor and Director of Finance Programs at Boston University Metropolitan College. Her research is focused on network theory and complexity science in macroeconomics, particularly the modeling of early warning indicators and systemic risk propagation throughout interconnected financial and economic networks. She is a co-editor of the book 'Econophysics and Sociophysics: Recent Progress and Future Directions' (Springer, 2017).

About the Series

Econophysics is a dynamic research field at the interface of physics and economics, in which analytical and computational techniques from physics are employed to study the properties of complex economic, financial, and social systems. Elements in Econophysics explores recent developments within this multidisciplinary research area and covers key topics including: big data in econophysics, financial networks, income and wealth distributions, market microstructure, stylized agent-based models, and sociophysics.

Cambridge Elements

Econophysics

Elements in the Series

Recurrence Interval Analysis of Financial Time Series
Wei-Xing Zhou, Zhi-Qiang Jiang, and Wen-Jie Xie

The κ-Statistics Approach to Income Distribution Analysis
Fabio Clementi, Mauro Gallegati, Lisa Gianmoena, Giorgio Kaniadakis, and Simone Landini

The Rise of Econophysics: A Connected History of Two Disciplines
Gianfranco Tusset

A full series listing is available at: www.cambridge.org/EECP

For EU product safety concerns, contact us at Calle de José Abascal, 56–1°, 28003 Madrid, Spain or eugpsr@cambridge.org.

www.ingramcontent.com/pod-product-compliance
Ingram Content Group UK Ltd.
Pitfield, Milton Keynes, MK11 3LW, UK
UKHW022307240426
470365UK00020B/500